The Four-Blocks®
Literacy Model

Writing Mini-Lessons for Second Grade:
The Four-Blocks® Model
by
Dorothy P. Hall,
Patricia M. Cunningham,
and Debra Renner Smith

Carson-Dellosa Publishing Company, Inc.
Greensboro, North Carolina

Credits

Editors:
Erin Proctor
Joey Bland

Cover Design:
Dez Perrotti

Layout Design:
Joey Bland

Artist:
Julie Kinlaw

ISBN 0-88724-814-4

Dedication

This book is dedicated to:

My husband, **David**, who loves me all the time.

My children, **Andrew** and **Ashleigh**, who are my heart's delight.

The **Renner family**, who encourage and support me.

My wonderful student teacher, **Kelwy El-Haj**, who encouraged me to pursue my dreams.

Dottie and **Pat**, who supplied the opportunity for my dreams to come true.

Deb Smith

All the second-grade teachers we have taught and talked about writing with, and have watched write. We not only thank you, but dedicate this book to you.

Dottie Hall, Pat Cunningham, and Deb Smith

Table of Contents

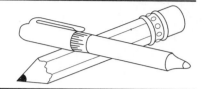

Table of Contents

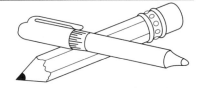

Introduction

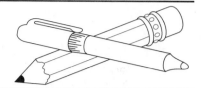

Writing Mini-Lessons for Second Grade

Writing is a critical part of a balanced literacy program for second graders. In second-grade classrooms, we see a wide range of writing. Some second grade teachers have children who write quite well. These children have written since kindergarten and have learned a lot about using language, grammar, and mechanics while writing. Other teachers look at the writing of their second grade students and realize they have a long way to go.

The wonderful thing about writing instruction is that it is a multilevel activity. When we allow children to choose what they want to write about and let them take as long as they need to finish their pieces, each child writes on his or her own level. As children continue to observe the mini-lessons and write every day, they become better at writing—regardless of their beginning points.

The major goal of the writing block is to teach children how to write. This is the time of the day in second grade when everyone writes. Children are learning to "talk on paper"—telling about the people they know, the places they have visited, the things they enjoy, their fears, and the things they have learned. Sometimes young children will write about things they won't talk about. When we read their writing we know that they are sharing their secrets with us! They tell **their** stories, whether real or made up! We teach children how to tell about the things that happen to them. We teach children to use their imaginations to go anywhere and do anything they like. We teach children how to tell us about their daily lives; how to write informational pieces, poems, riddles, and stories—with beginnings, middles, and ends. We help them to use correct grammar and mechanics as they write. We help them respond to reading by writing. We ask them to write and then write more. At some point, we teach them how to publish so that they have a reason to add on, write more, rewrite, revise, and edit. We want all children to see themselves as authors. We let second graders share their writing with their classmates each day and, often, have a celebration with family and friends at the end of the year.

Reading and Writing in Four-Blocks Classrooms

In Four-Blocks second grade classrooms, we devote 30-40 minutes each day to each of the four major approaches to teaching reading. (For more information about Four Blocks, see *The Teacher's Guide to Four Blocks®* by Cunningham, Hall, and Sigmon.) During the Self-Selected Reading Block, the teacher reads aloud to the children and then children read books that they choose. This is the time when, with the teacher's help, children select books at their own levels—books they can and will read. While the children read, the teacher has individual conferences with children about their self-selected books. (For more information about Self-Selected Reading, see *Self-Selected Reading the Four-Blocks® Way* by Hall, Cunningham, and Gambrell.)

Writing Mini-Lessons for Second Grade: The Four-Blocks® Model

During the Guided Reading Block, we focus on comprehension while we guide the children's reading in a variety of texts. We use many before, during, and after reading strategies so that all children will gain the skills and strategies they need to learn to be better readers. We give the children the support they need to read and understand grade-level texts. (For more information about Guided Reading, see *Guided Reading the Four- Blocks® Way* by Cunningham, Hall, and Cunningham.)

During the Working with Words Block, we teach children how to read and spell high-frequency words and the letter-sound patterns needed to decode and spell other words. (For more information about Working with Words, see the *Month-by-Month Phonics for Second Grade* by Hall and Cunningham.)

During the Writing Block, children write and share each day and they observe the teacher writing and thinking about writing during the daily writing mini-lesson. The Writing Block serves a dual function.

Children who have limited literacy skills have the opportunity to use writing as an approach to learning to read. As the year goes on and children develop more reading skills, the focus of the Writing Block shifts to helping children become better writers.

The mini-lesson is critical to the success of the Writing Block and the focus of the mini-lessons changes as we proceed through the second-grade year. We have divided the mini-lessons in this book into three sections: Early in Second Grade—Getting Started, Most of Second Grade—Continuing to Grow, and Later in Second Grade—Getting Better.

Mini-Lessons for Early in Second Grade—Getting Started

Early in second grade, we emphasize writing as putting down on paper what you want to tell. During the mini-lesson, we think aloud about what we want to tell them and then we write it. As we write, we think aloud about all the things authors have to think about as they write. During the first few weeks of school as the children write, we circulate around the room and encourage the children. We don't spell words for them but we help them stretch out words and we point them to places in the room where they can find the correct spellings of words.

After 15 to 20 minutes of writing time, we let several children share their writing. Early in the year, we gather the children in a group and have them tell what they were writing about. Later, we begin using the more formal Author's Chair. In most classrooms, $1/5$ of the children are designated to share each day. The children read one piece they have written since their last sharing day—or a finished piece— and then call on other students to tell something they liked and to ask questions. Most teachers establish writing folders or writing notebooks for children and they keep all their first-draft writing in these notebooks or folders. They check daily to see that each day's writing has the date. The date is necessary to see the progression of the children's writing.

Mini-Lessons for Most of Second Grade—Continuing to Grow

For most of the year, we are teaching second graders how to write and how to get better at writing. Editing and learning to use an Editor's Checklist are important components of how children learn to become better writers. We begin an Editor's Checklist with an item or two and the children edit the teacher's writing each day for the items on the checklist. Before putting away their writing each day, we ask the children to do a quick edit of their own writing for the items on the checklist. We add to the items on the checklist gradually, taking our cue from the children's ability to edit for the items already on the checklist.

When the children are comfortable writing and no longer need us circulating and encouraging, we establish the publishing procedures. In most classrooms, children pick one piece to publish when they have three to five good pieces written. The teacher's time, which has been spent circulating and encouraging children in their writing, is now allocated primarily to writing conferences in which the teacher helps children revise, edit, and publish. Once publishing begins, not all children are writing first drafts during the writing time each day. Some children are working to produce the three to five good pieces from which they will pick one to publish. Some children are conferencing with the teacher and preparing to publish. Other children are copying or typing and illustrating their published pieces.

Once children begin publishing, we do mini-lessons in which we teach some simple revision strategies and we teach the children to peer edit.

For most of second grade, we encourage the children to write about whatever topics they choose in whatever form them choose. We do, however, include some focused writing weeks in which we teach the children how to write within particular forms and on particular topics, and how to write a story or summary with a beginning, a middle, and an end. During these weeks, students may learn how to use a web or a paragraph frame to organize information and write a report, and how to write a friendly letter. Sometimes, we compile their focused writing into class books and duplicate these books so everyone takes home a copy to read over and over again.

Mini-Lessons for Later in Second Grade—Getting Better

Later in second grade, we continue to focus our mini-lessons on areas where children's writing shows us we need to reteach. We work more on revising and editing. We include some focused writing weeks and often help children write poetry and personal narratives. The stories that we have been writing about our lives are really personal narratives. Third graders are often required to write personal narratives during locally- or state-mandated writing tests! Many second-grade teachers point out to their students that they have been writing personal narratives all year in second grade. If you have not been publishing, remember this is an important skill. Publishing gives children a reason to revise, edit, and rewrite. Having a Young Authors' Celebration will give the class a chance to celebrate all their wonderful work as writers and young authors this year.

The Mini-Lessons

Doing a good mini-lesson every day is critical to the success of the Writing Block. The mini-lesson is your chance to show children how to do all the different things writers do. It is essential not only to keep the mini-lesson brief—8 to 10 minutes—but to also do some writing. It is crucial to avoid just talking through the lesson. Before, during, and after writing, we think aloud about what we are doing. This allows the children to see how we make all the decisions a writer must make. We think aloud about what to write and how to write it:

"Let's see. What do I want to tell you today? I could tell you about what I did this weekend—or I could write about the time my dog got lost. I know! I will tell you about what we will be studying this month in science."

We think aloud about our spelling strategies:

"I can look at the Word Wall to spell **favorite** because we just put it up there last week. I can stretch out alligators—**al-li-ga-tors**. I can spell **Tuesday** because it is on the calendar. I can spell spent because I know it rhymes with the word wall word, **went**.

We think aloud about punctuation and capital letters:

"This ends my sentence and it is an exciting sentence, so I will put an exclamation mark. I start my next sentence with a capital **F. Charlotte** needs a capital **C** because it is the name of a city."

We think aloud about revising and adding on:

"This is the piece I began yesterday and didn't have time to finish. I will reread what I wrote yesterday to get my brain thinking again . . . I am going to change **fun** to **exciting** because it was really exciting to watch the Olympics, and that is more descriptive than **fun**."

We do many different mini-lessons focused on the same writing strategy and we return to strategies taught previously when we observe something in the children's writing on which they particularly need to focus.

Once we begin an Editor's Checklist, we have the children do a quick check of our writing each day for the items on the list. When we start modeling adding on and writing a piece across several days, we wait until we have finished the piece and then use the day's mini-lesson to have the class edit the entire piece for the items on the list.

We do mini-lessons on how to select a piece to publish. On these days, the children are not watching us write but they are watching us look at, and think aloud about, which of several pieces we most want to publish. Once we have chosen a piece to publish, we do a mini-lesson in which the children help us do some simple revisions and then we reedit the whole piece. We do mini-lessons in which we show the children how we turn an edited piece into a published book. They watch us go through the stages of deciding how much to put on each page, carefully copying or typing the pages, illustrating the pages, and assembling the book.

How to Use this Book

Because it is impossible to know how many mini-lessons are needed for each focus, we have included one full mini-lesson and then a lot of possibilities for other lessons. These other ideas can be done immediately, or they can be revisited weeks later when observations of the children's writing indicate that certain lessons need to be reviewed and retaught to the children.

Across the years, we have observed that teachers who have the most successful writers in their classrooms do a mini-lesson faithfully every day in which they model and think aloud about every aspect of the writing process. In fact, we have concluded that the quality, variety, and explicitness of the mini-lessons usually distinguishes teachers who enjoy the Writing Block from those who don't. We have tried in this book to capture the spirit and essence of all the excellent second-grade mini-lessons we have seen and to share them with you so that you and your children can feel happier and more successful with writing.

Early in Second Grade–Getting Started

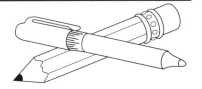

Early in second grade, we emphasize that writing is putting down on paper what you want to tell. As the children begin to write, we provide one-on-one help to our most struggling children. We ask them to whisper their sentences to us or we ask them what they want to tell and help them construct simple sentences. We then help them stretch out the words in that sentence and point them to words on the Word Wall and on other print displays. If necessary, we help them put a finger space between words and we ask them to read their sentence back to us pointing to each word as they read. This individual coaching of our most struggling writers each day makes a remarkable difference in their ability to get a sentence written that they can read and talk about.

We also pay some attention to our advanced writers, reading what they have written with them, marveling at how well they used the print resources in the room and stretched out words and at the fact that they wrote five whole sentences or filled up a whole piece of paper! Writing is the most multilevel of all the four blocks. With your help, all children can write a sentence and your advanced writers can write many sentences.

It is important to take some time early in the year to just write before beginning the publishing cycles. Once we begin publishing, we use the time while the children are writing to circulate around the room helping them revise, edit, and publish. The encouragement and individual coaching you are able to do while you circulate early in the year gets everyone off to a good start and assures that every child knows what is expected during the daily writing time.

To start with, we have an informal sharing time each day. We gather the children in a group for sharing and comment on all "the interesting things they thought of to tell." We call on particular children to share and marvel at all their good writing ideas.

"Bobby wrote about his bike. Read to us what you have written so far about your bike, Bobby. Cherisa wrote about her dolls. She has ten of them! They all have names. Read what you have written about your dolls, Cherisa. I had lots of dolls when I was your age and they all had names, too. I might write and tell you about them tomorrow."

When the children are comfortable writing and are writing longer pieces, we begin using an Author's Chair. One by one, each child reads one piece he or she has written since their last sharing day. After each child reads, he or she can call on other students to tell something they liked and to ask questions. The teacher models "nice" comments and good questions and the children soon learn to enjoy their time in the spotlight.

On the following pages are some of the mini-lessons we do early in second grade. We do as many of each as our particular class needs. We come back to lessons done earlier if we notice that some children need to have that strategy reviewed.

Mini-Lesson Focus: Modeling How to Write Using Think-Alouds

The first day of school many teachers wonder, "How well do the children in my class write?" To find out, teachers often get a writing sample. Some teachers assign children a topic such as, "Write about your summer vacation," or "Write about yourself." Some children begin quickly, while others think, "I didn't go anywhere!" or "I don't know what to write about me." In the Four-Blocks model, teachers don't assign topics (except during focused writing lessons). Children need to learn that writing is putting down on paper what you want to tell. Think-alouds are a great way to get second graders to understand that writing is telling. They also show how and what writers think when they write.

The teacher says:

"Since I am your new teacher you don't know a lot about me; but you will soon know more. Today I am going to write for you and tell you about me."

The teacher thinks aloud and writes:

"I begin my sentence with a capital letter." (Does each thing as she says it.)

My name is Mrs. Smith.

"I put a capital at the beginning of **Mrs**. and **Smith** because names always begin with capitals. I end my sentence with a period because telling sentences always end that way."

I have a husband named David Smith.

"I begin this sentence with a capital letter. **Have** is one of the words on the Word Wall. (Looks at the Word Wall as she writes **have**.) **David** and **Smith** each need a beginning capital letter." (Continues to do each thing as she says it.)

I have a dawter and a son.

"I begin this sentence with a capital. **Daughter** is a hard word for second graders to spell and when a word is hard to spell, you can stretch it out and write the sounds you hear." (Stretches out and writes "**daw**," then pauses, stretches out and writes "**ter**.") "I end my sentence with a period."

Their names are Ashleigh and Andrew.

"I begin this sentence with a capital. I know how to spell my daughter's and son's names and remember to use capitals at the beginnings of their names. I end my sentence with a period." (Continues writing and thinking aloud about capitals and periods.)

I live in a brown house. I drive a green car.

"**Brown** is over there with the color words and **green** is another color word."

I teach second grade at South Haven Elementary School.

As she writes, the teacher thinks aloud about the process she is using. She models and talks about using capital letters and periods. The teacher also uses this opportunity to str-e-tch out a word or two that the children do not know how to spell and to show how to use the print in the room to spell words. Because she thinks aloud as she writes each day, more and more children will come to understand and use the processes she models and talks about. After her mini-lesson, the teacher has the children write what they want to tell her. Many write about themselves, but some write on other topics.

Other Ideas for Modeling How to Write Using Think-Alouds

Using Literature for Modeling Think-Alouds

Read *How I Spent My Summer Vacation* by Marc Teague during the teacher read-aloud part of Self-Selected Reading. At writing time, begin your mini-lesson by saying, "This morning I read *How I Spent My Summer Vacation* and you wanted to tell me about your summer vacation. So, I thought to myself, 'When it is writing time I am going to tell the class about my family's vacation.' The story I read was a made-up story but my story is true. Here is how I spent my summer vacation."

> In June, as soon as school was out, my family and I went to Dizney Wurld. We flew to Florida. We went . . . .

Remember to think aloud and tell the children about the capital letters you use and why, the words you stretch out (because they are hard for many second graders), and what you put at the ends of the sentence and why as you tell your vacation story, real or made up.

Beginning Capitals and Periods

In some mini-lessons, you will want to focus on one particular part of the writing process. You can think-aloud focusing on beginning capitals and periods. Write something and think aloud only about the use of capital letters and periods.

"Today I am going to write about second grade. I will begin my first sentence with a capital **S**."

> Second grade is the best grade. In second grade we . . . .

"I end my first sentence with a period and begin my next sentence with a capital **I**."

Toward the end of your lesson, stop and ask children what you should put at the end of your sentence and what kind of letter you need to begin the next sentence.

"This is the end of my sentence. What do I need to put here? What kind of letter should I use to start my next sentence?"

Capital Letters for Names and I

Write something and only think aloud about how you capitalize names and I. Toward the end of your lesson, stop and ask children what kind of letter you should use to begin names and I.

"This weekend I went to my grandmother's house. All my family was there because it was her birthday. Today I am going to write and tell you about my grandmother's birthday party."

> I ("I is always a capital letter when it is a word.") went to my grandma's house yesterday. I ("Another capital I.") saw my sisters, Susie and Rebecca, there. ("I start **Susie** and **Rebecca** with capital letters because they are names.") We went there for her birthday party. Grandma was 84 years old! Ashleigh and Andrew could not believe the candles on her cake. She got presents from Susie . . . .

When you get to a name or the word I, ask the children what you should do. Let them "help" you by telling you that names and the word I need a capital letter. You can even share the pen and ask a child to come up and write that word.

Mini-Lesson Focus: Writing a Good Sentence

Writing a good, complete sentence is not an easy skill to learn. Children need to learn what a good sentence is, and there is really no way to explain that. The best way to help all your children learn how to write good sentences is to do some early mini-lessons in which you write only one sentence and you talk with the children about what makes it good. A good sentence makes sense to the person who is hearing or reading it!

The teacher draws and says:

"Sometimes a picture helps people write. Here is my car. I am driving to my sister's house in Grand Rapids. I love to go and visit my sister."

The teacher thinks aloud and writes:

"Now I will write a sentence about my picture."

I went to Grand Rapids to visit my sister.

The teacher asks:

"Who is this sentence about?" (Waits for children's responses.)

"Where did I go?" (Waits for children's responses.)

"What did I do?" (Waits for children's responses.)

"Yes, this is a sentence about me. It tells where I went. I went to Grand Rapids. Who did I go to see?" (Waits for children's responses.)

"Yes, I went to visit my sister and her family who live there."

The teacher tells his students that he will walk around as they begin to draw.

He wants each of them to whisper to him the sentence they will write today before they write it. If a child says one complete sentence, the teacher tells him, "That is a wonderful sentence," and moves on to the next child. If children don't tell him a complete sentence, the teacher helps them say a complete sentence before they write. If they tell him several sentences, the teacher tells them that they have three good sentences and helps them find the end of each sentence as they say it.

The teacher has the children draw a picture and write a sentence that answers the questions: Who? Where? and What? He gathers the children in a circle, so that they can share their pictures and sentences.

Other Ideas for Writing a Good Sentence

Doing More Draw-and-Write-One-Sentence Mini-Lessons

Draw a picture of a pet and write a sentence about that pet.

This is my dog, Quincy.

Talk about your dog and read your sentence.

Ask: "What kind of pet do I have? What is my dog's name? Do you know someone with a pet?"

Circulate as your children begin to draw and write and have them whisper their sentences to you before they write. Help them to form good, complete sentences. Gather the children in a circle and have them share their pictures and sentences.

Drawing a Picture and Letting Your Children Help You Come up with a Good Sentence

Draw a picture of yourself doing something you like to do. Ask your class to help you come up with a good sentence to go with your picture.

Mrs. Smith likes to read books.

Circulate as your children begin to draw and write and have them whisper their sentences to you before they write. Help them form good, complete sentences. After writing, gather the children in a circle and have them share their pictures and sentences.

Rereading a Book with One Sentence per Page and Writing a One-Sentence Response

Show children a book you have recently read aloud that has just one sentence on each page. Re-read a few pages from the book and help children notice that each page has a picture and one good sentence. For the writing part of your mini-lesson, write one good sentence that summarizes the book. If the book you reread was *The Relatives Came* by Cynthia Rylant, your sentence might be:

Many relatives came to visit a family living in the mountains.

Writing a Sentence and Focusing on Finger Spacing Between Words

If your students are not putting spaces between words, focus your think-aloud on putting a finger space between words. Draw a picture of two "stick figure" friends and write a sentence identifying your friends.

These are my two friends, Pat and Dottie.

As you write, think aloud as you put a space between each word. "After the word **these**, I put a finger space before writing the next word **are** . . . ."

Mini-Lesson Focus: Expanding a Sentence with Questions

Keep in mind that at the beginning of the year in second grade, you have all kinds of writers. Your main goal is to encourage your students to write and get them self-motivated. It is very natural for some of your students to be writing "I like" stories. Be open to the writing such as: "I like my mom," "I like my computer," "I like my dad," etc. Let students enjoy their writing and be patient with them for a while. They will learn and grow as writers by watching you write each day during your mini-lesson. Mini-lessons on expanding a sentence will help move children forward in their writing.

The teacher says:

"I went to a great party this weekend. I had so much fun! I am going to write about that party." She builds up the anticipation by saying how exciting and wonderful the party was, then writes:

> I liked the party.

The teacher puts down the pen and says, "I'm done." She watches the children's mouths open and asks, "Does anyone have a question?" Of course, they have many, so she lets them ask their questions:

"Where was the party?"

"Who was it for?"

"What did you eat?"

"Were there any presents?"

The teacher tells her students, "When someone reads our writing, they often have questions. We should try to answer the questions that readers might have when we are writing."

The teacher writes, answering the questions and expanding on the first sentence:

> I went to a party at my sister Susie's house. She lives in Grand Rapids. We had a birthday party for Grant. Grant is 2 years old. We ate chocolate cupcakes. Grant got lots of presents. His favorite present was a truck. I liked the party.

The teacher talks about the questions they asked and the answers she wrote:

"The questions you asked me helped me to write more sentences about the party. Thinking about the questions that someone might ask you about your writing can help you write more. I am going to walk around the room as you write and ask you some questions to help you make your writing more interesting."

Other Ideas for Expanding a Sentence with Questions

Doing More Lessons Where You Write One Sentence and Say, "I'm Done!"

Write about going to a wonderful soccer game (or any sport in which your class is interested when you write this) or going to see a movie.

I saw a great soccer game (movie) last night.

Put down your pen and say, "I'm done." After a few seconds ask what they want to know. Continue writing and answer the children's questions in your next sentences.

The Titans and the Packers were the two soccer teams. They played at the . . .

Letting a Child Write a Sentence and Letting the Other Children Ask Questions

Have a student come up and write a sentence. (You might want to choose the student the day before; you can also prearrange the sentence you want them to write.)

I like to help my mom cook.

Once the student finishes the sentence and puts down the pen, let the other students ask questions: "What do you cook? How do you make it? How often do you cook with your mom?"

Let the student answer the questions. Then, depending upon the student, either you, or the student, write the answers to these questions.

I help my mom cook dinner. I like to bake cookies, brownies, ...

Choosing One Child's Sentence and Letting the Other Children Ask Questions

At the start of your mini-lesson pass out index cards and have each student write one sentence. Have them write something they would like to tell the class. Have the students return their sentences to you. Write one student's sentence for the class to see and read.

I got a new bike for my birthday.

After you have written the sentence, let the other students ask questions. Have the student who wrote the sentence answer these questions as asked. Do as many of these as you can in your 10 minutes. (This may be a week's worth of mini-lessons if your class needs it!)

It is the bike I have always wanted. It is a red dirt bike with . . .

Expanding a Sentence with Who, What, Where, When, and Why

Show the class a picture of someone you know and can write about. Show the five "W" questions (Who? What? Where? When? and Why?) to your class. They may be on a chart or glove (one question on each finger). Talk about the five "W" questions. Write the answer to each question as a complete sentence.

Zannie Murphy is my niece. This is a picture of her driving my boat. Zannie lives in California. Every summer she flies to North Carolina and visits me at my lake house. She likes swimming in the lake. She likes riding in our boat. We have fun at the lake!

Mini-Lesson Focus: Choosing a Topic

For many children, writing is easy once they decide what to write about. In Four-Blocks classrooms, teachers want children to view writing as telling. It is important to stress that when you write, you write about what you want to tell. During your mini-lessons, think aloud often about what you might want to "tell." As the children listen in on your thinking, they see how you decide what you want to tell and they get some ideas about what they might tell us. Following is what that mini-lesson might look and sound like.

The teacher says:

"I wonder what to write about today. I could write about the new game we learned yesterday in P. E. I could write about going to see *The Lion King*. I know. I think I will tell you about my dog that loves pizza."

The teacher thinks aloud and writes:

My dog, Quincy, loves pizza. So do I.

(As she writes, the teacher has the children read the words.)

My whole family loves pizza.

The teacher asks:

"Do you want to know what kind of pizza I eat?"

The teacher continues to think aloud and write:

Last night we got a cheese pizza from Pizza Hut.

The teacher rereads what she has written so far and then asks:

"Can you guess what my dog did?"

The teacher finishes her writing:

My dog, Quincy, loves pizza. So do I. My whole family loves pizza. Last night we got a cheese pizza from Pizza Hut. Quincy stole our pizza from the kitchen table. He ate it. Boy was I mad!

The children and the teacher read the writing together.

Then the teacher says: "Today, I wrote about a time my dog ate my pizza. I could have written about the new game we learned or *The Lion King*. But I decided to tell you about my dog and how he stole our pizza. What will you write about today?"

As the children are dismissed from the writing mini-lesson, they tell the teacher what they will write about today. The children listen to one another and those that didn't have an idea about what they wanted to write about, get some ideas when they hear the other children's. Taking a few minutes to dismiss children in this way actually saves time because most children begin writing as soon as they return to their seats.

As the children write, the teacher circulates and encourages children. She talks with them about what they want to tell, pointing out difficult-to-spell words on the Word Wall and other places in the room. The teacher helps the children stretch out words that are not in the room—but does not spell words for them!

Other Ideas for Choosing a Topic

Using an "I'm An Expert" Sheet

Remind the children that our best writing is always on topics we know about and care about. "Confess" that some days, you can't think of anything you really want to write about. Then, later in the day you think of all kinds of things. Tell the children that you are going to make a list of five topics you are an expert on. Let the children watch you make your expert list and then lead them in a discussion of what they know a lot about and have them make their individual expert lists. Here is one teacher's list:

I am an expert! I know all about:
1. My Dogs Shelby and Quincy
2. School
3. Disney World in Florida
4. My Family
5. Animals

Narrowing the Expert Topics

Remind your children that your expert topics are things you know a lot about. For this mini-lesson, list, next to each big topic, some specific things you might write about.

I am an expert! I know all about:
1. My Dogs Shelby and Quincy: How I Got My Dogs; What Quincy Likes to Do; What Shelby Doesn't Like to Do
2. School: My Students; Our Classroom; Books; Writing; Four Blocks
3. Disney World: Old Key West Resort; Grandparents Go to Disney World
4. My Family: David; Ashleigh; Andrew; Family Traditions
5. Animals: Dogs; Cats; Tigers; Lions; Whales; Endangered Animals

Of course, you can use your list to stimulate future mini-lessons.

Developing an Individual Topic List:

As you see children who have problems coming up with a topic, help them to make a list. At the beginning of second grade, many teachers interview these students, jotting down ideas on an "I am an expert sheet". This is what the interview might look like:

Teacher: "What do you want to write about?" Student: "I don't know."
Teacher: "What do you like to do?" Student: "Swim."
The teacher records **swim** on the expert sheet.
Teacher: "Where is your favorite place to eat?" Student: "At Grandma's."
The teacher records **grandma** on the expert sheet.
Teacher: "What did you do during vacation?" Student: "Went to the beach."
The teacher records **beach** on the expert sheet.

Next, read the list of three writing topics back to the student and say, "You are an expert! You know all about going swimming, being at Grandma's, or the beach. Which one are you going to write about today?" If the student chooses, **beach** ask some questions such as, "Tell me about going to the beach. What did you do? With whom did you go? When did you go?"

Mini-Lesson Focus: Writing Is Telling about Something

Lucy Calkins (1996) says that in Writer's Workshop, "Children write about what is alive and vital and real for them—and other writers in the room listen and extend and guide, laugh and cry and marvel." As teachers, you have to get that message to your children. Writing is simply telling about things that are important in people's lives. Writing is simply telling things on paper!

The teacher says:

"What can I write about today? Let's see. What do I know a lot about? I know about things that have happened to me. What has happened to me lately? Has anything interesting happened to anyone I know? I know! My daughter and I went shopping. Let me tell you all about it.

The teacher tells:

"My daughter Ashleigh is just a year older than you. She loves to read the American Girl chapter books. Ashleigh has all the books. We are now buying the dolls that go with each book. They cost a lot of money, so we buy just one doll at a time. You can only buy them at the American Girl Store. Last weekend, I took Ashleigh to the American Girl Store in Chicago. We drove to Michigan City. Next, we took a train to downtown Chicago. I bought Ashleigh a "Kit" doll. The doll looks just like the one on the cover of the book about Kit. She is wearing an outfit that matches the girl on the cover. Watch and read as I tell my story in writing."

The teacher thinks aloud and writes:

> I took my daughter Ashleigh to the American Girl Store in Chicago. We drove to Michigan City and then took the train to downtown Chicago. Ashleigh loves all of the American Girl books. She wants all of the dolls. I bought Ashleigh a Kit doll. The doll has an outfit on that matches the one on the book cover.

The teacher and the children read the writing together:

The teacher reads what she has written with the children and asks: "Can you see a picture of the story in your mind? This is a true story about something that happened in my life. Because I remember it, I can tell you about it and write about it. That's how writing is telling about things. Sometimes, we tell true stories and sometimes we use our imaginations to make up stories."

The teacher reminds the children, "The easiest and best way to write a good story is simply to tell a story from your life. All of us hear stories from our parents, our brothers and sisters, our neighbors, and our friends. When we write, we are telling stories on paper!"

Other Ideas for Writing Is Telling about Something

Reading Stories from the Lives of Other Children
Read a few stories written by children from a previous year, stories that have clearly come from their own lives. (Many teachers make copies of pieces they know they want to use in future lessons.) Ask where the writers got the ideas for their stories. Children usually quickly understand that these are events that really happened in the lives of the writers.

Next, ask your children why they think each writer chose that specific time to write about? They will usually answer that it was a special time, or a time that was really important to them for one reason or another. It might have been a time when they had strong emotions. They may have been very excited, scared, happy, or sad.

Finally, ask why they think these writers remembered so many details about this time in their lives. Help children understand that when something makes you have strong emotions or feelings, you don't even have to think about trying to remember it. It's in your mind and heart to stay. And that's why telling a story from your life is the easiest way to write. All of the details and events are already in your mind.

Finding the Stories in Your Life

Make a list of five things from your own life that would make good stories to tell. Read this list with your children and pick one of them to write about today.

> My Horrible, Terrible Morning
> My Funny Friend CeCe
> Shopping in Chicago
> My New Computer
> Painting Andrew's Room

Helping Children Find Their Stories

Have children brainstorm things that have happened to them that they think they will probably never forget. Make a list with some children's names and their ideas.

> Jake—my new baby brother
> Tess—learning to ice skate
> Sam—my new computer

Some children may want to start a list in their writing folders for future reference. "Story Topics from My Life."

Using Ideas from Books Read-Aloud
Remind children of a book you have recently read aloud to them, such as *The Dance Man* by Karen Ackerman. Ask them where they think the author got the idea for this book. *The Dance Man* was about the author's grandfather. He once danced on stage. Write a few sentences about what your grandfather can do, even if it is something very normal.

> My grandfather likes to fish. One time I went fishing
> with him . . . .

Mini-Lesson Focus: What to Do about Spelling (Using a Word Wall)

Young children like to write but cannot spell all the words they want to write. The high-frequency words (was, have, they, said, get, went, etc.) that they will write over and over again, are on the Word Wall. During the Working with Words Block, practice spelling these words. You should also do On-the-Back activities to help the children spell Word Wall words with endings and words that have the same rhyming pattern as Word Wall words. To get children in the habit of using the Word Wall when they write, do several mini-lessons that model how you use the Word Wall when you are writing.

The teacher thinks aloud:

"What could I write about today? I could write about riding on a bus or riding the train in Chicago. I could write about swimming in the pool at a hotel this weekend. I think I will write about swimming. We have been adding to our Word Wall each week. While I am writing, I will show you how I use the Word Wall to help me spell words."

The teacher thinks aloud, talks, and writes:

Swimming

I went ("**Went** is on the Word Wall. Who can tell me what color **went** is? When I want to write **went**, I look at the Word Wall. Word Wall words have to be spelled right!") swimming on Saturday. ("**Saturday** is not a Word Wall word but it is on the calendar. I can spell **Saturday** by looking at the calendar.") My children went with me. We stayed ("**Stay** rhymes with **play**. **Play** is on the Word Wall. I use the pattern **ay** and start it with **st**. Then, I add the **ed**. **Play** helped me spell **stayed**.") in the pool for 2 hours. The pool was ("**Was** is on the Word Wall. I can look there and spell it right.") warm. We were all wet ("I know how to spell **wet** because it rhymes with the Word Wall word **get**. I just have to change the beginning letter.") walking back to our room. We got cold!

The teacher reminds the children:

"As you are writing today, remember to use the Word Wall to spell Word Wall words and words with the same rhyming pattern.

Other Ideas for What to Do about Spelling

Using the Print in the Room to Spell Words

Write something and only think aloud about how you spell words. Stretch out a few of the longer words. Refer to the Word Wall and other print resources in the room. "Today I think I will write about a trip to the lake. I went to the lake this past weekend so it is easy to remember it and write about it!"

One ("Look at the number words to get the spelling of **one**.") August weekend, ("Look at a calendar to get the spelling of **August**.") my family went to the lake. It was a sunny ("Look at the weather words to get the spelling of **sunny**.") day. We saw many boats on the lake. They were green, blue, and white. ("The color-word chart helps me spell all the colors.") We . . . .

Reminding the Children of Word Wall Words Every Time You Write

I like to ride ("Which words in this sentence are Word Wall words?" "Yes, **ride** is a Word Wall word. I'll look over there and spell it right.") on the bus. I take ("**Take** is another Word Wall word. Can anyone tell me what color **take** is? How should I spell **take**?") the bus to the airport. I like (The teacher looks at the Word Wall, points to the word **like**, and says, "**Like** is on the Word Wall. I look at the word **like** and spell it correctly: l-i-k-e") to read on the bus. The bus . . . .

Stretching out the Words That Second Graders Can't Spell

The high-frequency words are on the Word Wall. There are also many other words in the room for the children to refer to—days, colors, numbers, etc. But many words children need are nowhere in the room. Encourage children to "sound them out" and write down the sounds they hear. You may tell second graders to do this, but you need to show them how.

I like to go to the mowntuns. (Stretches out the first part and writes **mown**, then stretches out the second syllable and writes **tuns**.)
We buy apple sider (**si-der**).

Mini-Lesson Focus: Author's Chair

Early in the year, sharing in second grade may be very informal. Call the children together after they write, make a circle, and let the children tell what they were writing about. As soon as the children get used to "the teacher does a mini-lesson and then I write," you want the children to have time to share their pieces and get feedback from the other students. When you think the children are ready, begin Author's Chair. In Author's Chair, children share one piece of writing and then ask the other students to make comments ("Say something nice," is the rule!) and ask questions. Most teachers designate $1/5$ of the children to share each day. Many teachers use a special chair (rocking chair, big stuffed chair, decorated plastic chair, etc.) for this, but any chair—or even a stool—will do! You can introduce Author's Chair to your students in a mini-lesson. For your mini-lesson, you can write about Writer's Workshop—what you will do each day and why.

The teacher talks about the class's daily writing time as she writes:

"Today I am going to write about what we do every day during Writer's Workshop. Every day I write for you; we call this our mini-lesson. During the mini-lesson, I talk and write. I talk about something you need to learn to become better writers. I write something I want to tell you."

Every day I write for you. We call this a mini-lesson.

"After I write, it is your turn to write. You return to your seats, take out your notebooks (or get your writing folders) and begin to write. What do I do while you are writing? Yes, I go around the room and visit or conference with some of you. We talk about what you are writing about."

Next, you write and I come around and conference with you. We talk about what you are writing.

"Usually we end our writing time by making a circle and sharing our writing. Starting today we will use this chair. (Shows the Author's Chair.) Everyone will be assigned a special day each week to share. I have made a sign to show who will share on which days." (The sign has Day 1, 2, 3, 4, and 5 and $1/5$ of the names are written after each day.) "On your day, you sit in our Author's Chair and read one piece that you have written since your last sharing turn."

From now on, we will end our writing time with Author's Chair.

"We will start Author's Chair today so if your name is after Day 1 (Reads the names.), look through your notebooks (folders), find a piece you want to read, and get ready to share. Today I will conference with those who will share today. You can each read your piece to me and we can talk about it and get ready for your first Author's Chair. (Together with the children, the teacher reads what he has written.)

The teacher is sure to conference today with those who will share in Author's Chair. After the children have written and the teacher has spent two to three minutes with each child who will share today, it is time for him to model the first Author's Chair "nice" comment ("I liked your story about you playing soccer. I am glad your team won!") and to ask the first question ("What was the score?").

Other Ideas for Author's Chair

Talking and Writing about What the Children Will Do During Author's Chair

Young children in second grade need to know what to do during Author's Chair. Writing about what they will do during Author's Chair will help some children understand the procedure. Talk and write about this.

> Every week you will get to share your writing in an Author's Chair. While sitting in the Author's Chair, the first thing you do is read your writing. Next, you ask for comments. What did the class like? They tell you. Then, you ask for questions. What does the class want to know more about? You will answer those questions. We will learn even more about writing!

Making a List of "Nice" Comments.

Children need to be told that when they share their writing they will hear "nice" comment first. If you have set this up during your circling and sharing, this will be an easy progression. Children aren't afraid to share in the Author's Chair if they always hear something positive immediately after reading their writing. Modeling this each day by making the first comment yourself is one way to assure that second grade children pick up this habit. Another way is to make a list of your comments and the children's comments that are appropriate. You can start this chart as your writing mini-lesson and then add to it every few weeks.

<u>Nice Comments from the Author's Chair</u>
"I liked your story about your bike. I didn't know you had a dirt bike."
"You must have had fun at the fair. You did so many things there."
"I liked the way you told us you rode the train to Chicago."
"I liked your fishing story. I have never gone fishing."

Making a List of Questions Children Can Ask during Author's Chair

Teach your children to ask appropriate questions during Author's Chair. Modeling this each day by asking the first question yourself is one way to assure that second grade children learn how to do this. Another way is to make a list of "good questions" and post the list in your room. Here is what a list might look like:

<u>Good Questions We Ask during Author's Chair</u>
"Where did you get the idea for this piece?"
"What is the setting of your story?"
"Can you tell us a summary of your story?" (first, next, last)
"Are you planning to add more to your piece?"
"Did you make this up or did it really happen?"
"How long did it take you to write this?"
"Where did you learn so much about____?"

Mini-Lesson Focus: Adding on to a Piece of Writing

Children need to learn how to add on to a piece of writing. Just like everything else you teach the children about writing, the most effective way to teach adding-on is to model it. Begin by writing a story one day—thinking aloud, talking, and writing. The next day, you can model how to revisit what you wrote, read over it, and add on to it. Taking two or three days to write about the same topic gives your children permission to do the same. Your most avid writers always have more to say than they can write in one day. Your struggling writers need more than a day if they are ever going to finish a piece! Encouraging children to take as many days as they need to write a piece is one way to make your writing block multilevel.

On the first day the teacher thinks aloud about her dog and writes:

Quincy

My dog's name is Quincy. He is a black lab. He weighs 90 pounds! He eats everything we give him, even food off the floor. We got Quincy when he was eight-weeks old.

The next day the teacher wants to add on:

The teacher revisits by thinking aloud, talking about, and rereading what she wrote. She takes out the transparency of (or turns the chart tablet to) the previous day's writing. "Now let's see. I started this yesterday. It was all about my dog Quincy. I wrote about how he looks and what he likes to eat." Read your writing with the children.

Then, the teacher says, "Did I tell everything about my dog? No, I have lots more to tell. I could tell how we got Quincy, who plays with him, and what they like to do together, there's a lot more to tell about Quincy. Today I am going to add on to my writing about my dog and tell you some more about Quincy." The teacher thinks aloud once again and adds on to her writing.

Quincy was a present to Andrew from my aunt and uncle. Andrew got Quincy a few years ago for his birthday. Quincy was just a puppy when he came to live with us. We walk Quincy every day. Some days, Andrew runs with Quincy down by the creek. Quincy likes to chase squirrels.

To finish, the teacher needs a third day:

The teacher still has not written all she wants to write about her pet and continues on another day—writing about a specific time. She begins by rereading her writing from the first two days and finishing her piece on the third day.

One day Quincy chased a squirrel up a tree. He . . . .

After writing each day, the teacher dismisses by task:

The teacher reminds children about adding on by dismissing them by task from the mini-lesson group, "Those who are still adding on to a piece can return to their seats and continue writing." The teacher waits while those children are seated. "Now, those who plan to start a new piece of writing can go back to their seats."

Other Ideas for Adding On to a Piece of Writing

Writing about Something That Happened to You and Stopping before the Ending

Think aloud and begin to write your story:

This morning I overslept. It was the start of a very bad day. My children were mad at me because I was hurrying them. I was supposed to make cupcakes for my son's class. I didn't have time. We had to stop at the grocery store and buy some. We didn't have time to walk the dog before we left home. I hope Quincy doesn't have an accident!

The next day reread your writing, then ask, "I started writing about a horrible day. Do you think I am finished with my story?" (Wait for the children's responses) "You are right, I just told you about my morning. I have to tell you what happened the rest of the day." Continue to write.

I got to school late. The principal was having a meeting with the teachers and I had to walk in late...

The next day you may want to finish the story and tell about what happened when you get home.

When I got home Quincy had made a mess...

Writing a Class Summary about a Story You Have Read in Guided Reading

Begin a summary of a story your class read during Guided Reading. Write the beginning one day.

This story begins with Arthur wanting a pet. He asks...

Add the middle the next day.

Arthur starts to take care of pets to earn money. He...

The end can be written on the third day.

Arthur gets his pet. He got a...

Sharing Students' Writing and Helping Them Add On

Make a transparency of a child's piece that could be added on to. Read the piece together as a class. Then, as a class, add on to the piece and finish it together!

Finishing a Story That Was Started during the Teacher Read-Aloud

After reading the beginning of a book too long to finish in one teacher read-aloud, write a summary of the story so far. The next day, ask your students how they think the story will end. Think aloud and write their ending. After you finish reading the book, compare the ending your class made up to the author's ending. Sometimes the children think their ending was just as good or better. Sometimes it is hard to top the original!

Most of the Year—Continuing to Grow

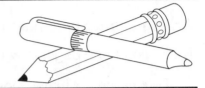

Once the children are all comfortable with the basics of writing some readable sentences that tell what they want to tell, we begin working on helping them improve their writing. Once Author's Chair is established, most second grade teachers begin helping children choose pieces to revise, edit, and publish. In most classrooms, each child picks one piece to publish when they have three to five good pieces written. The teacher's time, which has been spent circulating and encouraging children in their writing, is now allocated primarily to writing conferences in which the teacher helps the children where they need it. For many children, the teacher helps them revise, edit, and publish.

We begin an editor's checklist and children learn how to edit the teacher's and their own writing using this checklist. We teach children how to use the checklist in mini-lessons when new items are added and the children edit the teacher's writing each day for the items on the checklist. Before putting away their writing each day, the children are encouraged to do a quick edit of their own writing for the items on the checklist. Their editing is far from perfect. Often they think their sentences make perfect sense just the way they are. It is hard to end a sentence with appropriate punctuation and begin the next sentence with a capital letter when you are not sure about when one sentence ends and the next one begins. Staying on topic is difficult for many adults and impossible for some second graders. What is important about the self-edit is not that they do it perfectly, but that they get in the habit of doing it. As the year goes on, if you are resolute about making just a few mistakes each time you write and having children be your editors and find your mistakes, all your children will become better—but not per- fect—editors of your writing and theirs. We focus their attention on story writing—which for second graders is almost always a personal narrative—and show them how to have a good beginning, middle, and end.

As the year goes on, we continue to teach mini-lessons designed to help children find strategies for choosing a topic and spelling words. During Guided Reading lessons we teach that stories have a beginning, middle, and end. During writing mini-lessons we reinforce this by writing stories that have a beginning, a middle, and an end. During the Author's Chair we ask, "What happened at the begin- ning (middle or end) of your story?" Sometimes we focus our mini-lesson, making sure we start our story with a good beginning sentence or sentences that tell who, where, and when. During other mini-lessons we make sure we tell what happened and have all the events in the right order or sequence. The hardest part for many second-grade students is having a good ending, so occasion- ally in our mini-lessons we focus on writing a good ending or revising our story and writing a better ending.

Many children like to write about people and things that really happened. We show them how they can make a web and use it to organize an informational piece. Writing informational pieces, or nonfic- tion, requires different skills than writing stories. During Guided Reading we teach our second-grade students how to read informational articles. During our Writing mini-lessons, we show our students that writing informational pieces often requires that we organize the information and then write about it. This information often does not have a beginning, middle, and end—unless we are writing about someone's life—but it should include all the things you want the reader to know about the subject. So, instead of assigning second graders a report to write, we show them how we would write one. We gather information about the subject, take notes, organize the information using a web, and write the report using our daily mini-lessons to model these important steps and to show children just what we can do. We have learned that showing is far more powerful than telling children what to do. We often combine what we are writing about with what we are learning in social studies or science. Sometimes we combine these stories into a class book for all to see and read.

If you have state or locally mandated lessons to teach, especially grammar skills, the mini-lesson is the time to teach those skills. Just remember—model, model, model! The daily writing of your students should guide your mini-lesson needs when talking about grammar or spelling skills.

For most of the year in second grade, just as with the early mini-lessons, we do many lessons for each important strategy. We decide exactly what to focus on by looking at the writing of our children. We often return to the focus of a mini-lesson taught weeks earlier and review that strategy again when the writing of the children shows that although we taught it, many of them didn't learn it! The order that we present these mini-lessons is one possibility, but teachers who are most successful at teaching writing will attest that the most important determinant of what you teach and when you teach it is what your children need. The order and number of lessons you do with this year's class will not be the same as what you will do with next year's class.

Mini-Lesson Focus: Starting an Editor's Checklist

Once the children are in the habit of writing each day, you should start an editor's checklist. Add items to the checklist gradually and show the children how to edit their own pieces using the checklist. What you put first on the checklist depends on your students, your preferences, and your curriculum. Most second grade teachers begin their checklist with two items: number 1. Name and date (If the children write in a notebook they just need the date.) Many teachers tell students to write these two items from the first day of writing in second grade. Then, they add number 2. Sentences make sense. Here is a first mini-lesson to begin the Editor's Checklist.

The teacher says:

"Soon we will start publishing some of your writing. When we publish, we have to check our writing to make sure everyone can read it and it makes sense. People who check writing are called editors. We are all going to learn to be editors so we can edit our own writing and help each other edit. Editors always have a checklist of things to check for. We are going to begin our checklist with two items." (Writes the two items on a piece of chart paper labeled Editor's Checklist. The teacher discusses each item as she writes it.)

Editor's Checklist
1.   Name and date
2.   Sentences make sense

"Each day, after I finish writing, you will help me check to see that I remembered to put my name and date on my writing and to see if all my sentences make sense. I am going to write for you first and then you will be my editors."

The teacher writes, putting the name on, but forgetting the date and including two sentences that don't make sense.

Mrs. Smith

Today is Ashleigh's birthday. She eight years old. Her grandmother is baking her favorite cake. She is making a chocolate cake with pink icing. How many candles will she on her cake?

"Now, I need you to be my editors. Let's check for number 1 first. Did I remember to put my name and date?" Have the children notice that the date is missing. Add the date and put one check at the top to show you have checked for one item.

The children read each sentence and indicate whether or not each sentence makes sense:

The second sentence gets a "thumbs down" and the teacher inserts **is** so that the sentence makes sense. The last sentence needs the word **have**. When all the sentences are checked, a second check is put at the top of the page. Here is what the edited piece looks like:

Mrs. Smith   ✔✔   October 2, 2002

Today is Ashleigh's birthday. She is eight years old. Her grandmother is baking her favorite cake. She is making a chocolate cake with pink icing. How many candles will she have on her cake?

Writing Mini-Lessons for Second Grade: The Four-Blocks® Model

Other Ideas for Starting an Editor's Checklist

Ending Every Mini-Lesson by Having Children Use the Checklist to Edit Your Writing

Once you have begun your editor's checklist, use it **every day** until all the children become good at checking your writing for the items on the checklist. Use a different color marker to edit your piece so that the editing and check marks stand out. Each day make one or two errors for your children to correct. Leave your name off and have one sentence that doesn't make sense on one day. Just leave the date off on the next day. Have one sentence that doesn't make sense on the third day. Continue to make one or two errors each day and have the children find them. They will watch your writing very carefully and delight in finding your mistakes! Some teachers appoint a different child each day as the editor and have this child come up and lead the editing. The child asks the questions (Name and date?) and puts a check at the top of the page. The child then leads the reading of each sentence and the "thumbs up" or "thumbs down" response. With a little help from the teacher, the student editor fixes the sentence(s) that doesn't make sense and puts a second check at the top of the paper.

Teaching the Children to Edit Their Writing for the Items on the Checklist

After a week or two of editing your piece, most children are ready to look at their own writing and check for the things on the checklist. As the writing time is ending, tell children you want them to practice being editors today with their own writing. Many teachers hand out special red checking pens or pencils to help the children switch from writing to editing. Have everyone read number 1 on the checklist and check for their names and the date. If these are missing, they add them with their red pen and put a check on the top of their paper. Next, have them read number 2 and then read their sentences and give each sentence a "thumbs up or thumbs down." Do not expect them to do this perfectly. They often aren't sure where their own sentences end and think all their sentences make perfect sense! It is not reasonable to think that every child will be able to find and fix every sentence that doesn't make sense. It is reasonable to get them in the habit of rereading their sentences to see if they make sense so that they will find some of the most obvious errors.

Using a Variety of "Doesn't Make Sense" Errors in Your Writing

There are lots of ways to write a sentence that doesn't make sense.

You can **leave a word out**:

> We went to the museum. We dinosaur bones. We never knew
> dinosaurs were so big. We had to look up . . . .

You can **use the wrong word**: (Try to use one that the children confuse and will recognize. Often it is easier to say the right word and write the wrong word.)

> We went to the museum. We **was** dinosaur bones. We never
> knew dinosaurs were so big.

You can get distracted and **forget to finish a sentence**:

> We went to the museum. We saw dinosaurs. We never knew
> dinosaurs were so.

Mini-Lesson Focus: Adding to Editor's Checklist (Beginning Capitals)

Most second grade students know that sentences begin with capital letters. It is time to add something else to your Editor's Checklist when the children automatically read the teacher's writing for these two checklist items and when they are in the habit of checking their own writing. Here is a mini-lesson for adding another item to the Editor's Checklist.

The teacher says:

"You are becoming such good editors that I think it is time to add another item to our checklist. Here is another thing editors always look for when they are editing a piece of writing." (The teacher adds number 3 to the checklist and reminds the children that most of them know to begin sentences with capital letters but sometimes they forget.) "All sentences need capital letters at the beginning. When we write we need to make sure we begin every sentence with a capital letter."

Editor's Checklist
1. Name and date
2. Sentences make sense
3. Beginning capital letters

"Today, after I finish writing, you will help me check my writing for the three items on the list."

The teacher writes, leaving off two beginning capitals:

Mrs. Hall   October 16, 2002

My house was very crowded (Stretches out **cr-ow-ded**.) on Sunday. my sister, her huzband (Stretches out **huz-band**.) and their three children, Matthew, Karen, and Kristen came to visit. They brought their two dogs, Ozzie and Harry. The dogs stayed in the backyard most of the time. My sister and I cooked our favorite foods. we had a good time, but there were people and dogs everywhere!

"Now, I need you to be my editors. Let's check for number 1 first. Did I remember to put my name and date? Good, we can put one check at the top. Now, when we check the sentences we are going to check for numbers 2 and 3. Let's read my first sentence together. Show me a "thumbs up" if it makes sense. Now, show me a "thumbs up" if I remembered the capital letter at the beginning of this sentence. Good."

The children continue to read each sentence and give a "thumbs up" or "thumbs down" to indicate if the sentence makes sense. Then, they look to see if the next word begins with a capital letter and read that sentence. The second sentence gets a "thumbs up" for making sense but a "thumbs down" for a capital letter at the beginning. The lowercase **m** is changed to a capital **M**. The first letter of the last sentence is changed to a capital **W**. The edited piece has three checks at the top of the page.

Writing Mini-Lessons for Second Grade: The Four-Blocks® Model   © Carson-Dellosa CD-2418

Other Ideas for Editor's Checklist (Beginning Capitals)

Ending Every Mini-Lesson by Having Children Use the Checklist to Edit Your Writing

Continue to use your editor's checklist **every day**. Do not make more than one or two mistakes but include all the different possibilities on different days. Leave your name off and have one sentence that lacks a capital letter another day. The next day leave the date off and write one sentence that does not begin with a capital letter. Have one sentence that doesn't make sense on the third day. Cluttering up your writing with a lot of errors is confusing to many children who can't keep up with them all. If you only make one or two errors, they will pay close attention to your writing and notice your mistakes!

Teaching the Children to Edit Their Writing for the Items on the Checklist

After a week or two of editing your piece for the three items, tell the children that you want them to edit their own writing for all three items. They should continue to check for name and date and then read their piece one time stopping at each sentence and asking themselves if it makes sense and begins with a capital letter. Again, do not expect them to do this perfectly. If they are not sure about where their sentence ends, they won't notice that the next word does not begin with a capital. What you want is for the children to get used to rereading their pieces for these items. As the year goes on and your students help you edit your writing every day, their sentence sense will develop and they will become better and better at editing their own writing.

Writing and Letting a Student Be Your Editor

Tell your class about something, think aloud, and write. When you finish, call a student up to the front, give him a different colored pen and maybe an "editor's hat"—a visor with **Editor** written on it! Have the student do the "quick check" for you. Children, even second graders, learn to do what we do. You could write:

Mrs. Smith

Today we go to the auditorium. Officer Friendly is coming to talk to. He will talk to all three second-grade classes. he will come to our school four times this year. This is his first visit.

Let the student check each item. Name and date, a check goes at the top. When the five sentences have been checked for the next two items, two more checks are placed at the top.

Beginning Some Sentences with I and Beginning Some with Names

It is not too early for most second graders to notice that names start with capitals even though they are not always at the beginnings of sentences. So forget to capitalize a name or two once in awhile. Here is a story about a family and the teacher has modeled this—but left out one capital letter for the children to catch in the quick edit.

I have lots of sisters and brothers. Joyce ("I begin **Joyce** with a capital letter because it is a name and it is at the beginning of a sentence. I have two reasons to put a capital letter there.") is the oldest child in my family. The next is willy. I am in the middle. The youngest are Carol and Bobby. We are all friends even though we do not all live in the same place.

Mini-Lesson Focus: Adding to Editor's Checklist (Ending Punctuation)

Since most second graders know that sentences end with a punctuation mark, add this to your Editor's Checklist soon after you put the beginning capitals on it. It is easier to check for these two items at the same time. Every sentence begins with a capital letter and ends with a period, question mark, or exclamation mark. Then, look at the next sentence—does it make sense; begin with a capital; end with the correct punctuation mark? Second-grade students can become very quick and automatic at reading the teacher's writing with the Editor's Checklist for these three items. They need to be reminded at the end of the mini-lesson, and in individual conferences, to check their own writing each day just as they check yours.

The teacher says:

"You are becoming such good editors that I think it is time to add another item to our checklist. Another thing editors always look for when they are editing a piece of writing is the correct punctuation at the end of each sentence. All sentences need a mark at the end so we know the sentence is over. We use a period most of the time. But, when we ask a question, we use a question mark. When we say something very exciting, we use an exclamation point." The teacher adds number 4 to the Editor's Checklist.

Editor's Checklist

1. Name and date
2. Sentences make sense
3. Beginning capitals
4. Ending punctuation (. ? !)

"Today, after I finish writing, you will help me check my writing for all four items on the list."

The teacher writes, talking about the punctuation mark needed at the end of each sentence.

With the second and last sentence, the teacher forgets to put the period at the end of the sentence even though the teacher says that the sentences need a period.

Mrs. Hall   Nov. 2, 2002

I went grocery shopping yesterday. I wanted to buy a turkey for Thanksgiving Turkeys were on sale! I bought a big turkey for Thanksgiving and a little one to put in my freezer . . . .

"Now, I need you to be my editors. Let's check for number 1 first. Did I remember to write my name and the date? Good, we can put one check at the top. Now, when we check the sentences we are going to check for numbers 2, 3, and 4. Let's read my first sentence together. Show me a 'thumbs up' if it makes sense. Now, show me a 'thumbs up' if I remembered the capital letter at the beginning and punctuation mark at the end of that sentence. Good."

The children continue to read each sentence and give a 'thumbs up' or "thumbs down" to indicate if the sentence makes sense, begins with a capital, and if it has ending punctuation. The second sentence gets a "thumbs up" for making sense, and beginning with a capital but a "thumbs down" for ending punctuation. The period is inserted. The third sentence gets all "thumbs up." The last sentence simply needs ending punctuation. The period is inserted. The edited piece has four checks at the top of the page.

Other Ideas for Editor's Checklist (Ending Punctuation)

Focusing on "Telling Sentences" that End with Periods

Continue to write and use your editor's checklist **every day**. Do not make more than one or two mistakes but include all the different possibilities on different days. Some days just focus on "telling sentences" that end with periods. After your quick check, you can remind the students that all the sentences need punctuation.

Second graders like to read. The book fair is coming to school. We will get to visit next Monday. That is the time to look at books and decide which ones you want to buy. We get to buy books on Friday.

Focusing on Questions and Question Marks

Some days just focus on questions or "asking sentences" that need question marks at the ends. After your "quick check," you can remind the students that most of the sentences today were questions and needed question marks at the ends.

Thanksgiving is a holiday. There is no school. What you will do on Thanksgiving Day? Will you stay at home or visit someone? Will you eat turkey? What else will you eat for your Thanksgiving feast? Will you go to a Thanksgiving Day parade? Will you watch football?

(When you ask these questions, be prepared for children who want to tell you the answers. Don't be surprised if many children tell you the answers verbally and through their writing.)

Focusing on Sentences that Need Exclamation Points at the Ends

Some days, include several exciting sentences that need an exclamation point at the end.

Oh, no!   What fun!   This is great!   Happy Birthday!

Not Confusing Students by Putting the Wrong Ending Punctuation

Don't put the wrong punctuation mark; it often confuses children. It is better to leave off the ending punctuation mark and let the children decide which mark is needed. When you leave off ending punctuation, leave off all three marks (but not in the same lesson!). When the children notice that you forgot the ending punctuation at the end of a sentence such as, Who wants to be in the play, ask students what kind of punctuation you should use. Then, put the appropriate mark there.

Everyone will have a part in our play

Include sentences that need exclamation points.

Everyone will be a star

When you use all three types of ending punctuation in your daily writing, leave off all three types on different days, and let children help decide which one to use, most children become good at using the appropriate ending punctuation in their writing.

Mini-Lesson Focus: Adding to Editor's Checklist (Circle Misspelled Words)

In most classrooms children are learning so much about writing that they have to be reminded of some things they learned earlier in the year. They are also ready to learn how to do more. Spelling is one of those areas where many second-grade children need constant reminders of the different spelling resources available to them around the room. The print in the room has expanded and some has changed; especially the theme boards (words connected to themes that stay up while studying that theme). Although you have stretched out a word or two in most of your mini-lessons, some children may still need coaching to do this. The middle of the year is a time to review the Word Wall and other print in the room and to add a new item to the Editor's Checklist: circle misspelled words. These words are usually the ones we stretched out in previous mini-lessons.

The teacher says:

"We have been learning about winter and the changes that occur in winter. I am going to write about winter today!" The teacher talks, focusing on how to spell words, and writes as she talks:

Winter

("This is the name, or title, of what I am writing today. I know how to spell it because it is right there on our theme board.")

In winter (theme board) it gets colder. ("**Cold** is on the theme board, too. It is the word **cold** with the ending **er**.") We (Word Wall) wear jackets ("**Jackets** is on the theme board also.") and wul (The teacher stretches out **wool** and gets it wrong!) coats ("This is another theme board word.") to keep warm. Birds fly south in winter. Animals (theme board) hunt for food in winter. Some animals hibernate ("Another theme board word.") in winter. We play (Word Wall) inside ("I know how to spell **in**, and **side** rhymes with **ride**—a Word Wall word. I just change the beginning sound.") when it is cold. Not all places are cold in winter.

The teacher does a quick edit:

The teacher ends this lesson with a quick edit of items 1 to 4 and by adding number 5 to the checklist. She circles the misspelled word that she had to stretch out (**wul**).

Editor's Checklist
1. Name and date
2. Sentences make sense
3. Beginning capitals
4. Ending punctuation (. ? !)
5. Circle misspelled words.

The teacher reviews the different ways she used the print in the room to get so many words spelled correctly in her writing today. She is sure to emphasize that there are many sources of help in the room for spelling—using the theme board, using the Word Wall, and using words that rhyme with Word Wall words and have the same spelling patterns. She points out that words that need to be stretched out are words that need to be checked on when publishing: "Circle these words as a reminder to fix them if this piece is picked for publication."

Other Ideas for Editor's Checklist (Circle Misspelled Words)

Looking at First Drafts and Reteaching How to "Read the Room"

Are your children using the color words, number words, calendar, and theme boards? If their writing shows that they are forgetting to use the print in the room, do a mini-lesson emphasizing this. If things have changed and it is time for a new schedule to be written, write it for your mini-lesson. "Today I will write our new schedule. I know you can help me spell many of the words correctly by telling me where in our room I can find them."

Our Schedule ("Let me copy that word from the old schedule!")

Monday – Music at 10:30 ("I can copy that from the old schedule or I can look at the calendar to get the word **Monday** spelled correctly. I can find the word **music** on the old schedule—not under Monday but it is there. **Music** begins like **Monday**.")

Tuesday – Art at 1:00 ("Where can I find the word **Tuesday**?")

Looking at First Drafts and Teaching How to Write Names Correctly

Are the children in your class writing the names of their classmates correctly? If not, teach them to use the names on the Word Wall. Many teachers begin their Word Walls with the children's names. Other teachers have a special names board, with the names of the children and other important school people—often with accompanying photos. However you do it, you need to display all the children's names somewhere in the room and teach them to look there for the spelling of the names. Refer to these names when doing your mini-lesson.

Yesterday we acted out the story, Arthur's Pet Business. Mark ("I can spell **Mark** by looking at the names on my Word Wall. **Mark** is the second name under the **M**.") played Arthur. DeAynn ("I can spell **DeAynn** by looking at the names on the Word Wall also. Her name is under the **D**.") was Arthur's sister. D. W. Craig was Father ("I can spell **Craig** by looking at the names on my Word Wall. What letter is **Suzanne** under?") Suzanne was Mother. The people with pets were . . .

Looking at First Drafts and Teaching How to S-t-r-et-ch Out Words Children Don't Know

Some children are afraid to misspell words. (Maybe they have gotten this message from their parents or another teacher!) Tell them, "When I was in second grade, just your age, I couldn't spell all the words I wanted to write. Most seven-year olds can't! So what is the solution? When a word isn't in the room or on the Word Wall then you have to stretch it out and write what you hear. You can always use your "ear" or "sound" spelling! Str-e-tch-ing out words does not mean you repeat the sounds over and over. Stretching out words means you say them s-l-ow-ly and write the sounds you hear." When children write repeated letters, like **zzzzoo**, they are usually isolating the sounds—not stretching them out. In your mini-lessons, you can model how to stretch out words without isolating the sounds.

The Zoo

We are going to visit the zoo. We will see tigers (Stretch **ti-ger-s** out.) . . . and elefants (**el-e-fants**). The animals are not in cages but are separated (**sep-a-ra-ted**) by fences (**fen-ces**) and pits.

When you edit today you will circle **elephants**, a stretched out word that does not look right!

Mini-Lesson Focus: Choosing a Title for Your Writing

In Four-Blocks classrooms, we want children to view writing as telling. We stress that when you write, you write about what you want to tell. As the children begin to write, they often put a name or title on their writing. The teacher writes about the class's field trip and writes, "Our Field Trip." A child wants to tell about her bike and she writes, "My Bike," at the top of her paper. It's time to talk about titles and how we choose them—and when.

The teacher says:

"Let's see. What do I want to tell you about today? I could tell you about the new book I just bought. I think I will save that to read to you later today. I could tell you about the basketball game that I went to on Saturday. My favorite team lost so I don't think that would be fun to write about. I know! I will tell you about the pecan tarts I baked last night. I baked 40 of them!"

The teacher thinks aloud and writes:

"Since this is going to be about my pecan tarts I will write that first as my title." The teacher then writes **Pecan Tarts** at the top of her transparency (or chart paper) to begin her writing. Next, she thinks aloud about what she did, why she did it, and how to write it. "Every year at this time I make pecan tarts for my friends. My mother used to make them when I was little and I learned how. Pecans grow on trees and I now have a pecan tree in my yard. This is the time of year when they fall from the tree. You can find them in stores or at the farmers' market. This year we gathered three large brown shopping bags full of pecans. I thought to myself, 'It's time to make pecan tarts!' I will start my writing by telling that."

Pecan Tarts

My mother used to make pecan tarts for our family. Now, I make them for my family. I have a pecan tree in my yard. Every fall the pecans drop from the tree just as the leaves do. We gather the nuts and carefully crack them open. First, I mix the ingredeence (The teacher stretches that word out and spells it wrong.). Then, I pour the filling into little pie shells and bake them in the oven. When they are done, I devide (Stretches out **de-vide**.) them into two groups. I give some to my friends and save some for my family.

Teacher and the class read the story and talk about the title:

"I wrote the name, or the title, first. Sometimes you know what you will write about and you can put that on your paper at the beginning. Other times you have an idea but are not sure what a good title will be. You can wait until you have finished to see exactly what you have written then and come up with a title. After you finish writing, it is a good idea to reread your writing and ask yourself, 'Is this a good title for my writing?' Let's do that now."

"**Pecan Tarts** is one name for this piece. What else could I have named this? " The children give the teacher titles like these: **"Baking Pecan Tarts," "Pecan Tarts for My Family," "My Pecan Tree,"** etc. The teacher can let the class vote on the best title or she can decide which title she thinks is best. If she decides another name is better, she can change the title.

Other Ideas for Choosing a Title

Writing and Having the Children Think of the Title

Write about something you have done and have the children come up with three or four possible titles. Choose or vote on which is the best. Put that title at the top of your paper. You could write about going to a basketball game to see Michigan play against Ohio State and Michigan winning. The children give you these possible titles: "**Michigan Wins**," "**Michigan and Ohio State Play Basketball**," "**Michigan Beats Ohio State**," and "**A Great Game**." All the titles are good so you let the children vote to decide. They choose "**Michigan Wins**." You write that at the top of your piece.

Choosing a Title, Writing, Then Deciding the Title Needs to Be Changed

Choose a title such as: "**My Dog**." Write about your pet dog (or choose a student's pet).

My Dog

Quincy likes to chase squirrels. He chases squirrels down by the creek. He stops the squirrels from gathering acorns for winter. They stay up in the tree when Quincy barks at them. If the squirrels dare to come down, he chases them again!

Decide that this story is not all about your dog but about something your dog likes to do—he likes to dig. Brainstorm some different titles with your class. Some of the titles might be: "**A Squirrel Chaser**;" "**My Dog Quincy**;" or "**Squirrels Beware!**" Choose the one you or the class likes best. If it is "**Squirrels Beware!**," then draw a line through the old title and write the new one above it.

Choosing a Title for an Informational Piece You Write

Teachers often work with "stories" to choose a title, but they need to do this for informational pieces also. Write about winter and have the children title the piece.

Choosing a Title for an Informational Piece, Writing, Then Deciding the Title Needs to Be Changed

Choose a title such as: "**Winter**." Write about animals, birds, and people getting ready for winter. Decide that this is all about getting ready for winter. Brainstorm with your class new titles for this piece. Choose one you or your class like best. Draw a line through the old title and write the new one above it.

Writing about a Book You Have Read to the Class and Choosing a Title

Write about a book you have read during a recent teacher read-aloud. Focus on the characters. If you read *Alexander, Who Used To Be Rich Last Saturday* by Judith Viorst, you could write about how Alexander lost his money and how second graders would not make the same mistakes. Decide on a title for this story. It may be something like: "**How Alexander Lost His Money**."

Mini-Lesson Focus: Adding to Editor's Checklist (Capitals–Names and Places)

If most of your children can check for the current items on the checklist, it is time to add something new to the "Editor's Checklist." Many second grade teachers now focus their children's attention on capital letters for names of people and places. Because of your modeling, many of your students may be using these capitals. Here is the mini-lesson we might do to add this item to the Editor's Checklist.

The teacher thinks aloud and adds another item to the checklist:

"You are becoming such good editors that I think it is time to add another item to our checklist. Here is another thing editors always look for when they are editing a piece of writing." The teacher adds number 6 to the checklist and says, "Most of you know this and do this when writing. We use capital letters at the beginning of people's name and the names of places. When you write your names you begin with capital letters. My name is Mrs. Smith and I always begin that with a capital letter. The name of our school is South Haven Elementary and we always begin that with a capital letter. My favorite place to go is Disney World; we begin that with capital letters. When we write the name of people or places we use a capital at the beginning." (Adds number 6 to the list.)

Editor's Checklist
1. Name and date
2. Sentences make sense
3. Beginning capital letters
4. Ending punctuation (. ? !)
5. Circle misspelled words.
6. Capital letters for names and places

"Today, after I finish writing, you will help me check my writing for all six items."

The teacher talks and writes, leaving out one period and failing to capitalize Chicago and Jordan.

Mrs. Smith   December 12, 2002

The Bulls Play Basketball

Last weekend, Andrew and I went to chicago. We went to see the Bulls play basketball There was a large crowd even though Michael jordan is no longer playing for them. The Bulls were playing the Detroit Pistons. The game was very exciting because it was so close. The Bulls won!

The teacher and class do a quick edit:

The teacher and class read each sentence for the items on the list. The teacher helps the children notice that names of professional basketball teams like the **Bulls** and **Pistons** also need capital letters. The teacher might also mention capitalizing **I**.

Other Ideas for Editor's Checklist (Capitals–Names and Places)

Ending Every Mini-Lesson by Having Children Use the Checklist to Edit Your Writing

Continue to use your Editor's Checklist **every day**. Only make a few mistakes but include all the different possibilities in your different lessons. You might write about places where it snows a lot and the cities or states you mention would need capitals at the beginning.

> The weather channel had pictures of a big snowstorm around the Great Lakes. They showed pictures of cities close by like Chicago, gary, and hammond. The blizzard may be heading for . . .

Writing about a City or Place in the Mountains or Desert and Having the Students Edit It

> It snowed in the mountains (Some children might think that **mountains** needs a capital. Explain that if it were the name of the mountains, like Appalachian Mountains or Rockies, we would need a capital, but it is not necessary just for the word **mountain**.) last night. We will go to Boone this weekend. There is a great place to ski there. It is called Snow mountain. Have you ever been skiing there?

Writing a Weather Article about Your Area and Having a Student Be Your Editor

Think aloud and write about the weather, being sure to include place names:

> A cold front is coming from the west. It crossed the Rocky Mountains and moved across the plains. (Children should be reminded that this is not the name of the plains so it doesn't need a capital.) Snow is coming to the Chicago area and is going all the way to the great lakes (This name needs capitals.) . . .

Writing a Piece Using a Lot of Names and Having a Student Edit It

Write a story about the children in your class or neighborhood or the teachers at school leaving one or two without capitals. Do a quick edit noting the capital letters you used and the ones you forgot.

> Mrs. tillman sent me a picture of her children. She has a son named jimmy Lee and two daughters named Courtney and Emily. She talks about Jimmy Lee a lot. He is quite a character.

Explain that **son** and **daughter** do not need capitals but that **Mrs. Tillman**, **Jimmy Lee**, **Courtney**, and **Emily** do need capital letters because they are people's names.

Writing about a Book and Talking about the Author and Characters

When writing about a favorite book you will have to use lots of capital letters.

> One of my favorite books is Johnny appleseed by steven Kellogg. It is a legend about a man that planted apple seeds all . . .

Writing about Yourself and Reminding the Students to Capitalize "I"

Write about what you like to do. As you write, remind the students **I** is always capitalized.

Mini-Lesson Focus: Revision by Finding a Better Word

Good writing can often be made better by changing a few words. This is a revision step. Some second graders really enjoy doing this; others don't. Children who like words like trying to find better words. Another reason to teach second-grade children to find a better word is that they often use the same words over and over again in their writing. An example of this is when children write that something is nice or good. Modeling "finding a better word" is an easy mini-lesson and children who are ready for this skill will pick it up easily. After the mini-lesson, you will find some children doing this revision as they read their writing to you.

The teacher says:

"Sometimes when I am reading over my writing to make sure it makes sense, I see that I have used the same word over and over, or I might read a sentence and think of a better word to use in that sentence. I just cross out the word that I've decided not to use and write in the better word above it."

The teacher reads a piece she has written on a previous day:

The Nature Science Center

Our class went on a field trip to The Nature Science Center. We had to take the bus there. We walked around inside the building. We saw some animals. We went to the room to learn about space. We saw many exhibits. We walked around outside to see the farm animals. We learned a lot about science.

The teacher thinks aloud and models this process, crossing out some words and writing words she thinks will make the writing better:

The Nature Science Center

Our class went on a field trip to The Nature Science Center. We had to take the bus there. We walked around inside the building. We saw ~~some~~ snakes, birds, and other small animals. We went to the ~~room~~ theater to learn about ~~space~~ the solar system. We walked around outside to see the farm animals. We learned a lot about science.

The teacher suggests to her students that they might want to look at what they are writing and decide if they can find some better words and improve their writing.

Other Ideas for Revision

Ending "I Love" Stories

Some children have been writing "I love" stories for a long time. (In November: "My Family" I love my dad. I love my mom. I love my…. In January: "Winter" I love snow. I love making snowmen. I love ice skating. I love…. In February: "Valentine's Day" I love valentines. I love candy. I love….) Using a pattern helps some children write, but after doing this for a while it is time for children to move on. The best way to make children aware of this and help them change is to do a mini-lesson on this and start each sentence with something besides "I love…" Be aware that children may do this with **like** also!

Valentine's Day

I love Valentine's Day. ("I am not going to say 'I love pink and red,' but…") Everything is pink or red, two of my favorite colors. ("I am not going to say 'I love valentines,' but…") I make valentines in school. I buy valentines at the store. ("I am not going to say 'I love valentine candy,' but…") Valentine candy is everywhere. Will you get a box?

Finding a Better Word for an Overused Word

Another mini-lesson you can do in second grade is brainstorming words that you might use in place of overused words. An example of this would be to brainstorm better words for **said** such as: **called**, **shouted**, **exclaimed**, **cried**, **yelled**, **whispered**, **groaned**, **whined**, etc. Then, start writing and use these suggestions.

The boy shouted to his dog, "Here, Shelby! Come here!" When David got home he found lunch was not ready yet. "Oh, no," whined David. Then, he whispered . . . .

Describing What You Mean by "Nice"

Write about someone. Describe the person physically (height, hair color, etc.) Then, say that she is nice. Read your writing over and decide that the class does not know what **nice** means. Cross out **nice** and add details instead.

Vanessa is nice.
Vanessa is ~~nice~~ always polite. She always says, "Please," and "Thank You."

Describing What You Mean by "Good"

Write about something. Describe a lunch and say that it was **good**. Read your writing over and decide that you (and the class) do not know what **good** means. Cross out good and be more specific.

Lunch was good.
Lunch was ~~good~~ delicious. We had a sandwich, potato chips, apples, and chocolate chip cookies.

Reminding Students during Author's Chair

Revision is something that students can be reminded of during Author's Chair. Once a student has finished reading her writing say, "Could you tell us more about _____?" Then, suggest the author add those details during rewriting.

Mini-Lesson Focus: Procedures for Publishing

By now your second-grade students are in the habit of writing each day, have learned to "add on" to a piece, have learned to spend several days writing a piece, and have learned about revising and editing. Now, it is time for the part of Writer's Workshop that many children absolutely love—publishing! Publishing—which really means making writing "public"—gives children a reason to revise and edit. In second grade, many children want to publish everything. Most teachers find it easier and more manageable if the children don't publish every piece they write. In most classrooms, children are allowed to choose one piece to publish when they have three to five completed pieces. Once publishing begins, the teacher changes how she uses her time while the children write. Instead of circulating and encouraging, teachers spend longer periods of time conferencing and editing with children who are ready to publish. How do you do it? Once again, you model it!

Day One of Publishing

The teacher shows the class three pieces she has written, and says:

"I have written many pieces this year. I have written about the things I like to do, the places I have gone with my family, and the things we are studying about. Today I am going to look at three of the pieces I have written and decide which one I want to publish. When we publish in this class, we make a book. Then, we put the book in the book basket so everyone can read it. At the end of the year you get to take the books you have published home. Let's look at the three pieces I think are my best." The teacher then puts three pieces on the overhead projector (or show three pieces from her chart tablet).

The teacher reads and discusses each of the three pieces:

One by one the teacher displays and reads each of the three pieces and discusses what she likes about each piece. "I like this one called "**Pecan Tarts**." I think it would make a good book and I know just how I will illustrate the pages. I really liked the story "**Ashleigh Visits the American Girl Store**" but I am not so sure everyone liked it as much as I did. I liked "**Getting Ready for Winter**," too. I want to publish something that most of the class would like to read. It is very hard to choose but I think for my first book I will choose "**Pecan Tarts**."

The teacher returns to the chosen piece and revises and edits it:

"The first thing I want to do is to decide if there is anything I want to change about my piece. I like it so I don't want to change much, but read it with me one time and see if you can think of anything that would make it a little better." The children and teacher read "**Pecan Tarts**" together and decide to add the word **front** before **yard**. The teacher makes a caret (^)and adds **front** before yard. The piece has already been edited but there are more items on the checklist now than there were at that time. The children and teacher do a quick reedit. The teacher circles two words that she had stretched out to spell. She then writes the correct spelling above these. "On the first draft, we don't worry about the spelling of words not displayed around in the classroom," she reminds them. "But I will help you fix the spelling of every word when you are making a book. That way, everyone can read it easily."

Day Two of Publishing

The first publishing lessons take more than one day to model. The first day should be spent choosing, revising, and editing the piece. The following day, model what comes next. This lesson should be completed on an actual book and the children should be close enough to be able to see what is being done. First, divide the piece into sections according to how many pages you have to write on in your book. Next, copy the book over in your "very best handwriting." (Some teachers may choose to edit with the child and then type the text.) Allow the children to read each sentence aloud as it is being written in the book.

The teacher thinks aloud, and writes the title page:

"I start with the title page and very neatly write the title here: **Pecan Tarts**. Underneath the title I write the word **by** and then write my name, **Mrs. Smith**, because I am the author of this book. You will write your name because you are the author of your book.

The teacher writes one sentence—in her best handwriting—on each page.

As a rule of thumb, the teacher never goes over ten pages for second-grade books. Some pages may have several lines of writing on the page if a student has written over ten sentences.

Page 1– My mother used to make pecan tarts for our family.
Page 2– Now I make them for my family.
Page 3– I have a pecan tree in my front yard.
Page 4– Every fall the pecans drop from the tree just as the leaves do.
Page 5– We gather the nuts and carefully crack them open.
Page 6– First, I mix the ingredients.
Page 7– Then, I pour the filling into the little pie shells and bake them in the oven.
Page 8– When they are done, I give some to my friends and save some for my family.

Day Three of Publishing—Illustrating the Book

On the third day, the teacher should model how to illustrate the book. The teacher turns to each page, thinks aloud about what she might draw, then draws a picture that goes with the text on the page.

My mother used to make pecan tarts for my family.

"On this first page I should draw my mother making pecan tarts and my family—but I should draw us how we looked long ago when I was young like you! On the next page . . . ."

Day Four of Publishing—Making the Cover, Putting the Book Together, and Reading It

On the fourth day, the book should be put together with a cover and read aloud. The title and author should be written on the cover and the cover illustrated. The teacher talks about the complete book and how carefully she copied over every page. Some children will write the final draft just like they wrote the first draft so stress that they copy the edited copy! Keep some correction fluid on hand for children if children write final copies in pen. If they type on the computer, remember to check it before they print.

Day Five of Publishing—"All about the Author" Page

On the final day of publishing, complete a mini-autobiography. Tell about the author by writing a page about yourself.

Mrs. Smith teaches second grade. She has a husband, a daughter, and a son. She likes to read. She likes to write books, too!

Let the children know that you will interview them and write this page when they publish their books.

Mini-Lesson Focus: Writing a Story (Beginning, Middle, End)

Remind your students that when you read aloud a story to them, the story has a beginning, a middle, and an end. During Guided Reading, the stories they read have beginnings, middles, and ends. This lesson focuses their attention on writing "stories" with a beginning, a middle, and an end. (This could also be a lesson in writing a summary if that is a skill you think your second graders need. A summary needs a beginning, a middle, and an end.)

The teacher says:

"I could write a story about visiting my sister who lives in the desert. My airplane trip would begin that story. I could write about a baseball game I watched. I know how that story would end—with my favorite team winning. I could write about one of my favorite books, *My Great-Aunt Arizona*. Since we are talking about stories having a beginning, a middle, and an end I will write about the book, *My Great-Aunt Arizona.*

The teacher thinks aloud and writes:

The teacher talks about the capital letters, ending marks, spelling, and what happened at the beginning, middle, and end (it may take three days to do this!) as she writes:

My Great-Aunt Arizona

This book, by Gloria Houston, is the story of her great-aunt Arizona. The story begins when Arizona is born in a cabin in the Blue Ridge Mountains. We learn about what her life when is like at home and at school when she is young

When Arizona grows up she becomes a teacher. She teaches in the one room school where she and her brother went to school. We learn what she looks like, what she wears, and what she teaches her students.

The story ends when Arizona gets married and moves to a new school down Henson Creek. There she has a daughter, teaches fourth grade, and talks about faraway places she would like to visit some day. Arizona dies at 93 and never visits those faraway places. Today, Arizona travels in the minds of her many students.

(On the fourth day the teacher revises all three parts: changing a word or adding details. On the fifth day she does quick check and then discusses what happened at the beginning, middle, and end.)

The teacher does a quick check with the Editor's Checklist.

She adds a period to the third sentence. Next, she discusses what she wrote about the beginning at the beginning, what she wrote about the middle in the middle, and how she ended by writing about the end. (The teacher might want to take out a story map or call the children's attention to it. "You can use a story map to help you plan what you write!")

Story Map	
Characters	_____
Setting	_____
Beginning	_____
Middle	_____
End	_____

Other Ideas for Writing a Story (Beginning, Middle, End)

Writing about Something That Happened to You

A lot of times teachers write about events that happen to them or their children. Choose that familiar topic, think aloud, and write your story with a clear beginning, middle, and end. You will probably need to add on to your piece across several days.

The Ice Show (or circus, ball game, movie, museum, etc.)

Skaters on Ice came to Grand Rapids last weekend. I took Ashleigh and Andrew. We drove to Grand Rapids. We stopped to pick up my sister and her two children. They were excited just like us. We parked in a huge parking lot. We got a program and found our seats.

The next day write about the Ice Show.

The skaters wore fancy costumes and . . . .

The third day write even more about the Ice Show (circus, ball game, movie, museum, etc.)

On the way home . . . .

On the fourth day you may want to revise all three parts by changing a word or adding details.

On the fifth day you might want to do a final edit.

Writing about One of Your Students

Have a private conversation with the student before you begin to write. This story allows you to review capitals for names and places.

Zannie's Trip to Disneyland

Zannie went to Disneyland with her mother, father, and brother Marc. They drove to the coast from their home in the desert. They stayed at the Grand Resort Hotel near . . . .

At Disneyland, they rode all the children's rides. They went to some shows . . . .

On the ride home Zannie fell asleep! Her mother and father had . . . .

Letting the Class Help You Construct a Story Based on a Book They All Know and Enjoy

Review a favorite book such as *The Three Billy Goats Gruff* or *The Relatives Came*. Let the class help you decide on new characters (perhaps some of the children!) and some new events. Write important details—including beginning, middle, and end—on a story map. Let the class help you write the story across several days of mini-lessons.

Mini-Lesson Focus: Reviewing Ending Punctuation Using Think-Alouds

Modeling how to write using think-alouds is one of the best ways to get your students to understand the writing process. We do this almost every day during our mini-lesson. When focusing on the punctuation that ends different types of sentences, think-alouds are a good way to do it. The children have observed the teacher putting periods at the ends of sentences that tell, question marks at the ends of questions, and exclamation points at the ends of sentences that show excitement. The children have edited for correct ending punctuation. When you see several students not using correct ending punctuation in their writing, it is time for a review mini-lesson that focuses on this.

The teacher thinks aloud and writes:

"Today as I write I am going to talk about the different punctuation marks I put at the ends of my sentences when I write. Sometimes I tell something like, 'Yesterday, I went to visit my sister in Grand Rapids.' Watch as I write that sentence."

Yesterday, I went to visit my sister in Grand Rapids.

"I begin with my sentence with a capital. I use the Word Wall to spell **went**. I stretch out and write **sister** because it is not a Word Wall word and not any place in the room. I put a period at the end of that sentence because periods go at the end of sentences that tell something."

"Sometimes I ask questions when I write. Can you guess what we did in Grand Rapids?" Write:

Can you guess what we did?

"When I write a sentence like that I begin with a capital, use the Word Wall and the print in the room to help me spell words. (The teacher models this.) When I get to the end I put a question mark because I have asked a question."

"Sometimes I write a sentence about something exciting. My sister had a surprise planned!"

My sister had a surprise planned!

"When I am writing about something exciting or surprising, I still begin the sentence with a capital. I still use the Word Wall, other words in the room, and stretching words for spelling, but I end with an exclamation point."

The teacher adds sentences and thinks aloud about the different ways she ends each of these sentences.

"I am going to add some sentences to my writing" (The teacher writes each sentence, discusses what punctuation she needs at the end and then puts it there.)

We went to Mrs. Tillman's house. ("This sentence **tells** where we went, so I put a period at the end of the sentence.")

My family and friends were all there! ("This sentence lets you know I was **surprised** that all my friends were there, so I put an exclamation point at the end of this sentence.")

Did you know yesterday was my birthday? ("This sentence asks a **question** so I put a question mark at the end of that sentence.")

Other Ideas for Reviewing Ending Punctuation Using Think-Alouds

Putting Periods at the Ends of Sentences That Tell Something

In some mini-lessons, you want to focus on one particular kind of sentence. The first kind of sentence that children learn about is the sentence that tells something. It ends with a period ("stop sign"). Here are some think-aloud examples focusing sentences that tell something.

We are studying about magnets in science. ("This needs a period.")

Magnets pick up metal. ("This needs a period.")

Magnets pick up paper clips. ("This needs a period.")

Magnets pick up thumb tacks. ("This needs a period.")

Magnets do not pick up paper or plastic ("What do I need to put here?")

Putting Question Marks at the Ends of Questions

"Sometimes we ask questions in our writing. When a sentence asks a question it needs a question mark at the end. Here are some questions that may be in our writing."

Who was this story about? ("This needs a question mark at the end.")

Where did the story take place? ("This needs a question mark at the end.")

When did the story happen? ("This needs a question mark at the end.")

What happened to the boy? ("This needs a question mark at the end.")

Why did he do that? ("This needs a question mark at the end.")

What did you think about this story ("What do I need to put here?")

Using Exclamation Points to Show Excitement

"When we want to show excitement we put an exclamation point at the end of the sentence we are excited about. Here are some sentences that we might want exclamation points at the end of."

I like New York City! ("This sentence shows some place I am excited about so I will put an exclamation point at the end of this sentence.")

Stars on Ice was great! ("This sentence shows an exciting place that I went to so I will put an exclamation point at the end of this sentence.")

We had so much fun! ("This sentence shows something I really liked so I will put an exclamation point at the end.")

My team just scored a goal! ("I am excited here because something good just happened. I will put an exclamation point at the end of this sentence.")

That is unbelievable ("What do I need to put here?)

Mini-Lesson Focus: Writing an Informational Piece (Using a Web to Organize)

Often when teachers and second graders think about writing they think about writing stories. When we write about things we are learning about or things we know a lot about they are not really stories. We call them informational pieces. Informational texts are not structured in the same way that stories are. Writing informational pieces is different from writing stories. We focus on how to write an informational piece in this mini-lesson.

The teacher thinks aloud about what to write:

"Sometimes I write about things we are studying in second grade. Sometimes you write about the things you know a lot about—like snakes or rocks. When people write about something and they want to make sure they include all the facts, they often start with a story web. A web helps organize the information. If I chose to write about Abraham Lincoln, a web would help me organize everything I know about him. If I chose rocks to write about, a web would help me organize what I know about rocks. Today, since we are studying and reading about dinosaurs, I am going make a web about dinosaurs and then use that web to write about dinosaurs."

The teacher starts a web, thinks aloud and writes:

Since I am going to write about dinosaurs, I will put that in the middle. I want to tell when and where they lived, what they ate, their body parts, and about the different kinds of dinosaurs we have studied. So I will put those four words in ovals around the corners. (She makes a web as she talks.)

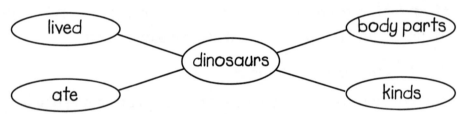

The teacher adds to the web, as she thinks aloud and writes:

She talks about where and when dinosaurs **lived** as she fills in that "spoke" of the web. The teacher talks about the **body parts** of a dinosaur which is the next "spoke" she fills in, remembering to mention that some dinosaurs had parts that made them different from one another (Triceratops). The teacher talks about the third "spoke" what dinosaurs **ate**. When she gets to the final "spoke," she adds the names of all the **kinds** of dinosaurs her second graders know. When she finishes the web, she reads and reviews it with her students.

Other Ideas for Writing an Informational Piece

Using a Web to Write Informational Pieces

Use the web you created to structure an informational piece about dinosaurs. Show the children how to write a beginning sentence about the topic. Then, include information from each spoke of the web to organize the information.

Dinosaurs

Dinosaurs lived millions of years ago. Some dinosaurs lived on land and some lived in the water. Their brains were small but their bodies were huge. Some dinosaurs had two legs and some had four. Some dinosaurs looked like huge birds and had wings. Some dinosaurs ate plants and some ate meat. There were many different kinds of dinosaurs, like tyrannosaurus, iguanadon, and triceratops. Dinosaurs were amazing animals!

Use a Paragraph Frame to Write about What You Learned

A paragraph frame is another way to organize information and write. The teacher creates the frame. Each child writes a paragraph, finishing the sentences with the information that child chooses. Children who struggle to write often experience success with the structure of paragraph frames and are proud of their finished pieces.

Dinosaurs

I learned that dinosaurs lived _____. I learned that dinosaurs ate _____. Some dinosaurs I learned about were _____, _____, and _____. The most interesting thing I learned was _____.

Making a Web to Write about a Person's Life

Create a web about a person (Lincoln, Washington, Martin Luther King, Jr., or a professional or Olympic athlete). Use the web to write an informational piece, showing the children how to write a sentence about the topic and then use each spoke of the web to organize the information.

Martin Luther King, Jr.

Martin Luther King, Jr. was born in Georgia. He grew up in a segregated wurld (Stretch this out and write what you hear.). He became . . . .

Making a Web about an Informational Book You Read and Writing from that Web

After reading an informational book (about insects, plants, birds or any other topic you study in second grade), create a web. Then, write an informational piece showing the children how to write a sentence about the topic (insects) and how to use each spoke of the web to organize the information.

Insects

We are learning about insects. We learned that insects have . . . .

Mini-Lesson Focus: What to Do When You Are "Stuck" ("I ain't got nothing to write about!")

Some children always have something to tell the teacher and the class and have no trouble coming up with writing topics. Other children find it harder to think of topics to write about each day (or every few days when they add on and don't write about something new each day!). If we can get children thinking about the many things they do each day or the many things they know a lot about (sometimes more than the teacher!), writing is easier. Giving topics is not the solution! It causes new problems—problems for the children who know nothing about that topic. In Four-Blocks classrooms, we stress that when you write, you write about what you want to tell. During our mini-lessons, we often think aloud about what we might want to "tell them today." As the children listen in on our thinking, they see how we decide what we want to tell them and they get some ideas about what they might tell us. Here is what a mini-lesson might look and sound like when you have kids that are "stuck."

The teacher says:

"Let's see. What do I want to tell you about today? I could tell you about my new "teacher sweater" and where I got it. I could tell you about the game show I watched on T. V.—it was wonderful because I knew all the answers! But, today, I want to write a story I thought of yesterday during Self-Selected Reading. Joe was sharing *Arthur Makes the Team* by Marc Brown with me during our conference. Joe was telling me how he was practicing hitting a baseball with his dad every night. He wants to play Little League this spring. I thought that would make a wonderful story. Joe could be the person in the story, not Arthur. Joe could tell us what he does and why.

The teacher thinks aloud as she writes:

> Once there was a boy named Joe. He was just about your age. Joe wanted to play Little League baseball. He was old enough to play and his brother had played when he was in second grade. Joe not only wanted to play on a team, he wanted to be a great player! Every night in his backyard, his father would pitch the ball and Joe would practice hitting. He was hoping to be one of the best hitters in Little League. But he was scared and worried, "What if I do all this practice and I can't hit the ball when I play in a real Little League game?" He had to become a great hitter! He had to hit a home run for his team. The more Joe worried, the more he practiced.

The teacher and children think aloud about other inspiring books:

"Can any of you think of books that might inspire you to write a similar story? What about *Magic Tree House* books? Where could the Magic Tree House take you? Could you write a story about someone like Junie B. Jones? Have you ever lost something important like the girl in *Missing: One Stuffed Rabbit*? Can you think of a book that helps you write a story?"

Other Ideas for What to Do When You Are "Stuck"

Thinking Aloud about a Few Topics You Don't Normally Write About

Think aloud about two or three topics you don't normally write about. Let the children know that just because you don't use those topics doesn't mean they can't!

"I could write about my neighbor hitting my mailbox with her new car and how she had her husband buy me a new one—and he painted it the wrong color. Boy, was she upset! I could write about my daughter's new video game. When we play she always wins. I am not as fast as she is. But I think I will write about Abraham Lincoln. We have been reading books about him and talking about him all week and even I learned some new things.

Abraham Lincoln was born in a log cabin. He worked hard to learn to read . . .

After you finish say, "Now most of you don't have a neighbor who hit your mailbox but you may have been in some other kind of accident, like on your bike or scooter. Most of you have video games you like to play and all of you know a lot about Abraham Lincoln. You all have many topics that you could write about even if that is not the same topic that I choose to write about. I wonder what you will write about today. I'll be roaming and reading before I begin my individual conferences."

Making and Keeping a Running List of Writing Topics

Make a list on your chalkboard or on a piece of paper. Let the children start their lists inside their notebooks or writing folders. Any time a new topic idea comes up, write it on this class list.

Things to Write About
1. My friends
2. A favorite book
3. A favorite time with Grandma (Grandpa)
4. Getting glasses (new shoes)
5. Michael Jordan (Tiger Woods? Any interesting person!)

Rereading the First Part of a Favorite Book (Don't Finish!), Then, Writing Your Own Ending

Reread the beginning of *Miss Nelson is Missing*. Get inspired and have your students help you! "The children in this second grade class have a substitute. What happens? How would you write the ending to this story? Help me to write another ending."

Miss Nelson is missing from school one day. A substitute named Laura Grump shows up. "I am your teacher today," she says.

Making a List of Places You Can Write About

Talk about the places you go to or would like to go to. Make a list for your mini-lesson one day. Choose a place on that list to write about during another mini-lesson.

Places I Could Write About
1. New York City
2. Charlotte
3. The Farmer's Market

Mini-Lesson Focus: Adding to Editor's Checklist (Stays on Topic)

Are the children becoming quick and automatic at reading your writing for the items on the checklist? Are most of them in the habit of checking their own writing for these items? Once most of your children can edit for most of the things on the checklist most days, it is time to add another item to the Editor's Checklist! "Staying on topic" is something most second graders need on their checklist. Following is a mini-lesson you might do when adding "stays on topic" to the Editor's Checklist.

The teacher says:

"You are becoming such good editors that I think it is time to add one more item to our checklist. Most of you do this already. When we write, we try to write about the topic we have chosen. Sometimes, writers include things that they are interested in but have nothing to do with the topic. That is another thing editors always look for when they are editing a piece. They look to see that everything the writer writes is about the topic." The teacher adds number seven to the checklist and says, "Number seven on our list is: stays on topic."

Editor's Checklist

1. Name and date
2. Sentences make sense
3. Beginning capital letters
4. Ending punctuation (. ? !)
5. Circle misspelled words
6. Capital letters for names and places
7. Stays on topic

"Today, after I finish writing, you will edit my writing for all seven items on the list."

The teacher writes:

She leave off one period, stretches out and misspells a word, and writes a short sentence that is not on topic.

Mrs. Cunningham   February 22, 2003

George Washington

George Washington lived a long time ago. The United States belonged to England at that time George Washington lived on a farm in Virginia. He was a general during the Revolutionary War when we won our independense (stretches out and writes **in-de-pen-dense**) from England. He was the first president of the United States. Do you remember all the presidents? George Washington had a big job of setting up a new government.

The teacher and the class do a quick edit:

The teacher adds a period to the second sentence, circles **independense**, and crosses out the sentence (**Do you remember all the presidents?**) that doesn't stay on topic.

Other Ideas for Editor's Checklist (Stays on Topic)

Using "Thumbs Up" and "Thumbs Down" to Determine If Each Sentence Stays on Topic

Continue to use your Editor's Checklist every day. Do not make lots of mistakes but focus on the errors you see most often in your students' writing. When you add an item, make one mistake for that item each day until your children catch on. When deciding whether a sentence stays on topic, use an every-pupil-response signal: "Thumbs up if sentence stays on topic, thumbs down if the sentence does not stay on the topic."

What We Do at School

We learn Math. (thumbs up) Our teacher reads to us every day, then we read. (thumbs up) We write every day. (thumbs up) We have lunch in the cafeteria every day at noon. (thumbs up) We all like video games. (thumbs down) In science we have learned about electricity, magnet, dinosaurs, and insects. (thumbs up)

Writing a Story and Adding a Sentence That Is Not on Topic

Write about someone in your class or something the children in your class like to do. Add a sentence that is not on topic. Read it as a class and do a "thumbs up" or "thumbs down" for each sentence staying on topic.

Andrew Plays Soccer

Andrew likes to play soccer. He is on a soccer team. He practices every day after school. He is a good at math. In one game, Andrew scored the winning goal . . . .

Writing an Informational Piece and Adding a Sentence That Is Not on Topic

Write about something you are studying about or the topic of an informational book you just read. Add a sentence that is not on topic. Read it as a class and do a "thumbs up" or "thumbs down" for each sentence.

Electricity

Everyone uses electricity every day. Electricity allows us to have lights in our homes and lights on our streets and highways. Many people use electricity to heat their homes and cook their food. Some people use gas to cook. Just how does electricity do these things? That is what we are going to learn in second grade!

Writing about a Book You Read and Adding a Sentence That Does Not Belong

Write about a book you have read to your class or a story your class has read during Guided Reading. Add a sentence that is not on topic (did not happen in the book). Read it as a class and do a "thumbs up" or "thumbs down" for each sentence.

The True Story of the Three Little Pigs

The author of this book is Jon Scieszka. This is the story of the three pigs from the wolf's point of view. The wolf says it was all a misunderstanding. The wolf likes apples. The story begins with the . . .

Mini-Lesson Focus: Self-Editing and Peer Editing

Most second-grade children can learn to self-edit and partner edit. Once the teacher is editing with the class and the Editor's Checklist is growing, the teacher often gives the children their own Editor's Checklist to put inside their notebooks or writing folders. Each time a new item is added, the children get a new list. When children are finished writing they self-edit using the Editor's Checklist. Some second graders excel at self-editing while others don't do much better than they did on the first draft without someone's help. As one second grader (who hadn't done much editing) said, "I did the best I could!" We teach self-editing every time we let the children help edit our piece at the end of a mini-lesson. In second grade, we let children help each other edit and do a lesson in which we model peer editing.

The teacher reads and thinks aloud about revising the piece she has chosen to publish:

Mrs. Hall   March 8, 2003

My Cat Tommy

Once I had a cat named Tommy. He was a big gray Persian cat He was fat and furry. A hurricane was coming up the coast and weather was rainy and windy. Tommy was lost. I could not find Tommy in the house. I could not see him when I looked out the window. We were afraid he might get hurt. My husband was on his way home from work. He saw Tommy stuck in the storm drain and reskood him. He dug him out of the debree, picked up the wet cat, and brought tommy home to us.

"Let's read my story together and help me think about revising it." The class likes the beginning of the story but thinks the sentence, **Tommy was lost**, needs to be moved after the sentences about not being able to find him. The teacher agrees and does this. The class thinks **soaked** would be a better word than **wet** and the teacher agrees and changes this. The class wants a better ending and helps the teacher come up with: **We were so happy to have our cat again!**

The teacher chooses a child to be her partner and help edit her writing.

The child takes a red marker and edits the teacher's writing using the checklist.

"Number one: It has the name and date. I put the first check at the top."

"Number two: All the sentences make sense. A second check."

"Number three: Do all the sentences begin with a capital letter? Yes, another check."

"Number four: One of the sentences we added needs a period at the end." The editor adds this and then puts a check at the top.

"Number five: Are the misspelled words circled? Yes, the misspelled words **reskood** and **debree** are circled." The editor puts another check on top and since this will be published, the teacher writes the correct spelling of **rescued** and **debris** above these words.

"Number six: The name **Tommy** in the last sentence needs a capital letter." The editor fixes this and then puts a check at the top.

"Number seven: The sentences all stay on topic and a final check goes at the top."

Writing Mini-Lessons for Second Grade: The Four-Blocks® Model

Other Ideas for Self-Editing and Peer Editing

Continuing to Do a "Quick Edit" of the Teacher's Writing as Each Piece Is Written

Often when visitors come to our Four-Blocks second-grade classrooms, they are shocked to see how well most of the children write and self-edit their pieces. Many children automatically include ending punctuation and beginning capitals on all their first-draft sentences. People and place names almost always have capital letters. When children finish writing, they automatically reread each sentence, referring to the checklist and fixing a few things that they notice need fixing. "How do you get this to happen?" the visitors regularly ask. The answer is simple yet crucial. Once the teacher introduces the Editor's Checklist, she leads the children to use it to edit every piece of her writing. When the teacher writes a piece that is finished in one day, the piece is quick edited the same day. When the teacher is writing longer pieces that take several days to write, the piece takes longer to edit. For longer pieces, the teacher usually uses the entire mini-lesson time on the day the piece is finished to let the children revise and edit it. Children love to be the teacher's editor and find her mistakes. This daily practice is the "magic potion" that produces so many competent second-grade writers.

Doing a Class Editing of a Student's Writing

Let a child who is getting ready to publish revise the piece with the class's help. Have the class use the checklist to edit the child's piece just as they edit the teacher's writing.

Doing Lots of Lessons in which You Choose Someone to Be Your Editing Partner

Children love being given the red marker and being the teacher's editing partner. Choose some of your "natural editors" to do this job as everyone watches. Some teachers buy a special visor and write **Editor** with a black marker across the front of the visor. The child who edits get to wear the editor's visor. Be sure to express your appreciation for their help in making your piece so much more readable.

Partnering your Students and Letting Them Edit Each Other's Writing

Pair your children and let them edit each other's writing. Partner children of similar writing abilities. This is not something that is done in most second grades until late in the year. However, if the children have been heavily exposed to helpful modeling, they are usually eager to be wonderful editors!

Mini-Lesson Focus: Writing a Friendly Letter

Writing a friendly letter is a task that many second-grade children are asked to do. In a Four-Blocks classroom, when we work on learning to write a particular genre, we call this a focused-writing lesson. Focus on writing letters and have each child write a letter. When the children finish their letters, they return to their self-selected topics. Children write better letters when they have a "real" reason for writing them. When a student moves, the teacher might model this process by writing a friendly letter to the student and then letting each student write a letter.

The teacher talks about the parts of a letter using a transparency of Lucy's letter:

"Here is a letter from Lucy who moved last week. She sent this letter to Jamie her good friend. Jamie let me make a copy. Let's look at the parts of Lucy's letter." The teacher talks about the date, how to write the date (**March 12, 2003**), the greeting, how to write the greeting (**Dear Jamie,**), the body (which contains the message about moving into a new house, having her own bedroom, and finding a good tree for climbing in her backyard), the closing (**Your Friend,**), and signature (**Lucy**) pointing to each part and talking about that part as she reads the letter. The teacher shows the letter:

Dear Jamie,   March 12, 2003

We moved into our new house on Saturday. It is a big, white house. I have my own bedroom now. There is a climbing tree in the backyard. I have not met any new friends. I miss you. Write soon!

Your Friend,

Lucy

The teacher pretends she is Jamie and models how to write a letter.

She thinks aloud about what she is doing as she put today's date and begins with the greeting **Dear Lucy**. The teacher writes a message (whatever she wants to tell Lucy about something that has happened at home or at school lately), and chooses a closing (discussing several choices the children might use), and then signs this letter with Jamie's name.

Dear Lucy,   March 20, 2003

We were so glad to hear from you. We are watching your old house to see if anyone moves in. We wonder if the new family will have children. Tell us all about your new school. What is your new teacher's name? Do you do Four Blocks there? I miss you. Write again!

Your Friend,

Jamie

The teacher does a quick edit and reviews the parts of the letter as well as the items on the Editor's Checklist. Then, the teacher has each student write a letter to someone they choose.

Other Ideas for Writing a Friendly Letter

Writing a Thank-you Letter

When your class has returned from a field trip, or the principal has invited a guest to school it is a good time to write a thank-you letter. Review the parts of a letter: date, greeting, body, and closing. Then, write a letter with the class, discussing what you want to say and why. Have the children write their own letters and be specific about what they enjoyed. If possible, gather some interesting stationery for the children to write their final copies on.

Dear Mr. Parker,   March 22, 2003

Thank you for inviting Gloria Houston to visit our school. We had never met an author of a book we read. We enjoyed learning about how she writes her books. We liked being able to ask questions. We will never forget this day.

Sincerely,
Mrs. Smith's second-grade class

Writing Thank-you Letters after the Holidays

Writing thank-you letters to relatives and friends for gifts received is always appropriate. This gives children a "real" reason to write a letter and teaches them a social skill as well. Invite children to write thank-you letters. Review the parts of a letter as you model writing this.

Reading a Book about Letters and Writing a Letter

The Jolly Postman by Janet and Allan Ahlberg is a book filled with letters that a postman is delivering. Many teachers like to read this book during the teacher read-aloud and then discuss the letters during a writing mini-lesson. The letters are from storybook characters and illustrate many real reasons people write letters. Pick a character and have the class help write a letter to that character.

Dear Junie B. Jones,   March 24, 2003

We like your stories. You say the funniest things. Sometimes we were afraid you would get into trouble in kindergarten. We are glad you are now in first grade. We wonder what will happen to you next.

Your friends,
Mrs. Smith's second-grade class

The children could write to Stellaluna and tell her how much they enjoyed learning about bats. They could write to Curious George and tell him about a time they got in trouble for being curious. The possibilities here are endless.

Using Commas in a Letter

Talk about the commas in a letter calling attention to this punctuation mark as you write a letter.

March 24, 2003 "In the date we have a comma between the day and the year."

Dear Michael, "We put a comma after the name in the greeting."

Mini-Lesson Focus: Writing a Report

Second-grade teachers often do some focused-writing lessons related to the science or social studies topics being studied. Children write and illustrate their pieces and this writing is compiled in a class book. The book is added to the material available for self-selected reading. Children love reading class books. A focused-writing lesson often takes a week or more from start to finished book. Following is an example from a class doing a study of dinosaurs, a popular topic in any second-grade class.

Day One

The teacher thinks aloud, the class brainstorms, and the teacher writes:

The teacher tells the class they are going to take a week off from their individual writing to make a class book about dinosaurs (or other topic such as birds, plants, etc.). They have been reading about and studying dinosaurs and together they brainstorm the names of these prehistoric creatures:

ankylosaurus	stegosaurus	proceratops	triceratops
iguanodon	anatosaurus	apatosaurus	brachiosaurus
coelurosaurus	ornitholestes	allosaurus	gallimimus
hypsilophodon	diplodocus	deinonychus	scolosaurus
tyrannosaurus			

The children work in groups to come up with questions about dinosaurs:

The teacher tells the children that each one of them will become an expert on one dinosaur and write about it. The children are put into groups of three to four children, with a recorder in each group. Each group lists questions they should try to answer in their dinosaur reports.

When did your dinosaur live?

Where did your dinosaur live?

What did your dinosaur eat?

What did your dinosaur look like?

How big was your dinosaur?

What were their body parts?

How do you pronounce your dinosaur's name?

What makes your dinosaur special?

How did your dinosaur protect itself?

The children choose a dinosaur to research and write about:

Because she knows some dinosaurs will be more popular than others, the teacher asks each child to list five dinosaurs he would like to write about. She then assigns each child a dinosaur, assigning more familiar dinosaurs to some of the less able writers. She reviews the resources in the room (books, encyclopedias, computer, etc.) and talks about the library as another place to find more about their assigned dinosaur. The teacher chooses a dinosaur no one has chosen—a stegosaurus—to model this process.

Day Two

The teacher models writing some facts she already knows about her dinosaur, the stegosaurus:

Stegosaurus

armor plates   *spikes on tail*   *ate plants*

Each child writes some facts already known about his or her dinosaur.

The children begin researching dinosaurs.

They use books, magazines, encyclopedias, Web sites and whatever resources are available in the classroom and library. They take notes on large index cards.

Day Three

The children continue researching and writing facts. The teacher circulates and gives support to those who need it.

Day Four

The teacher thinks aloud and models writing her report:

Stegosaurus

Stegosaurus had armor plates on its back and a spiked tail. It ate plants . . . .

The children begin writing their reports, with help from the teacher as needed.

Days Five, Six, and Seven

The children continue writing and partner editing their reports using the Editor's Checklist.

The teacher does a final edit with each child. The reports are copied or typed and illustrated and put together into a class book.

Other Ideas for Writing a Report

Writing Reports Using Social Studies Themes

One second grade teacher did a month long Social Studies unit on Japan. During this time she encouraged the children to write about Japan and what they were learning. When the month was over, all but three children had done this! The teacher then sat down with these three students individually and helped them put on paper what they had learned. Many of the teacher's mini-lessons during that month were related to Japan

Japan

Japan is made up of four islands. It is a small country but it is crowded with people. The capital is Tokyo. People in Japan . . . .

Writing about Summer or the End of the Year

As the school year ends some children are excited about summer vacation (and some teachers too!). Capture that enthusiasm for summer and let the children tell you and their classmates about what they will do during this time. This is a class book that most children are really excited about making.

Lake Michigan

Every summer, we go to my grandmother's house on Lake Michigan. We like to go swimming in the lake. We like to ride in Grandpa's boat and see the . . . .

Later in Second Grade–Getting Better

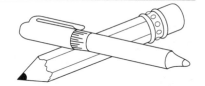

Later in second grade, we continue to teach mini-lessons that help children write better. We look at children's writing to know what we need to reteach and what will help move them forward in their writing. We focus more on revision and work with grammar as we help children choose more descriptive nouns, verbs, and adjectives.

For those teachers that feel their students have just begun to write, we suggest that you go back to some of the early lessons, and do them "one more time." You will find that students who were not ready to do the things you were modeling in the early lessons are now ready. Look at the writing of the students in your class and ask yourself, "What aren't they doing that most second graders can do? How can I help them? What do some (or many!) students need another lesson on?" The most important thing you can do for your second graders, regardless of their writing abilities, is to let them watch and listen as you write and think aloud everyday. The activities in this book will produce children who not only can write in second grade, but children who want to write each and every day!

The end of the year is always a good time to stretch your students. Other lessons we have not included in this book that second-grade teachers sometimes model are **Words in a Series Have Commas between Them** and **How To Use Quotation Marks When People Talk**. These two skills are usually discussed and modeled by the teacher in mini-lessons, but mastery of the skills is not expected in second grade and the items are not put on the Editor's Checklist. Not all second graders will become wonderful writers; but you should see growth in all students at this time of year when you compare their writing early in the year to what they are writing now.

April is poetry month and many second graders enjoy writing poetry—a nice change of pace for later in the year. Many second-grade teachers also do some focused writing lessons on stories and "how-to" writing. They also compile everyone's writing into a book that all the children take home as a souvenir of second grade. Ending the year with a Young Authors' Celebration gives everyone a good send-off for the summer. On the following pages are some of the mini-lessons we do later in second grade.

Mini-Lesson Focus: Teaching Grammar (Nouns, Verbs, and Adjectives)

There are mini-lessons in this book on revising by finding a better word (page 42) and replacing overused words (page 43). In this mini-lesson, the focus is on particular grammar elements—nouns, verbs, and adjectives—which are part of most second-grade language arts curricula. First, have the children identify the nouns, verbs, or adjectives. Then, ask them to think of more descriptive nouns, verbs or adjectives and replace some of the boring ones.

The teacher takes out a recent piece of writing containing some boring nouns and says:

"I was looking through some of my writing yesterday and realized I had used lots of boring nouns. I decided my writing would be much more lively if I replaced some of these boring nouns with more descriptive nouns. Let's read this piece I wrote about my garden when I was your age."

> When I was your age, we planted a big garden in the yard. We grew vegetables. My brother and I weeded the garden and picked off the bugs. My mom and I picked the vegetables. We also planted flowers. On Saturdays, we sold some things at the market.

The teacher has the children read the piece with her.

They identify the nouns—people, places, and things: **garden, yard, vegetables, brother, garden, bugs, mom, vegetables, flowers, things, market.** Then, the teacher changes some of the nouns (or adds to them) to make her writing more descriptive.

Here is what the piece with more descriptive nouns might look like.

> When I was your age, we planted a big garden in the backyard. We grew tomatoes, squash, corn, cucumbers and beans. My brother, Willy, and I weeded the garden and picked off the beetles. My mom and I picked the vegetables. We also planted flowers—roses, tulips, and daisies. On Saturdays, we sold some vegetables and flowers at the Farmer's Market.

The teacher suggests to the children that they may want to look at some of the nouns in their writing to see if they have used any boring nouns that they could replace with more descriptive nouns.

Other Ideas for Teaching Grammar (Nouns, Verbs, and Adjectives)

Doing the Find and Replace Lesson with Boring Verbs

Find (or create) a piece of writing that has boring verbs.

Camping Out

When I was your age, I went camping with the Girl Scouts. We went to the campground. We slept in a tent. We walked through the woods. We cooked hot dogs and beans. We cooked marshmallows and made s'mores with graham crackers and chocolate. We were hungry and the food was delicious. Camping out was fun.

Have the children read the piece with you and identify the verbs—**was, went, went, slept, walked, cooked, cooked, made, were, was, was**. Change some of the verbs to make them more descriptive. Your revised piece might look like this:

Camping Out

When I was your age, I went camping with the Girl Scouts. We drove to the campground. We slept in a tent. We hiked through the woods. We grilled hot dogs and heated beans. We toasted marshmallows and made s'mores with graham crackers and chocolate. We were hungry and the food tasted delicious. Camping out was fun.

Doing the Find and Replace Lesson with Boring Adjectives

Find (or create) a piece of writing with that has boring adjectives.

The Circus

The circus is coming to town. What will we see at the circus? We will see big elephants. The lion tamer will make the strong lions do good tricks. The acrobats will have pretty costumes and do scary tricks. The funny clowns will make us laugh. Every year, we have a nice time at the circus.

Have the children read the piece with you and identify the adjectives—**big, strong, good, pretty, scary, funny, nice**. Change some of the adjectives to make them more descriptive. Your revised piece might look like this:

The Circus

The circus is coming to town. What will we see at the circus? We will see enormous elephants. The lion tamer will make the mighty lions do amazing tricks. The acrobats will have colorful costumes and do dangerous tricks. The funny clowns will make us laugh. Every year, we have a terrific time at the circus.

Mini-Lesson Focus: Writing Poetry

April is poetry month! Poetry is one genre second-grade children are exposed to through teacher read-alouds and Guided Reading in Four Blocks classrooms. Most young children think poetry has to rhyme until they begin reading and writing poetry. When teachers share poetry written by favorite children's poets like Shel Silverstein and Lee Bennett Hopkins, children learn that poetry is concise, brings images and sounds to our minds, may be rhyming or not, and is usually about a topic or subject.

Writing a cinquain is a favorite of teachers and children. A cinquain consists of five unrhymed lines that are usually made up of two, four, six, eight, and two syllables. A simplified variation that is made up of one word, two words, three words, four words, and one word is easier for young children to write.

The pattern for an easy cinquain can be written as follows:

Line 1: One word that is the title (usually a noun)

Line 2: Two words describing the title

Line 3: Three words that show action

Line 4: Four words that show feelings

Line 5: One word, can be a synonym for the title

Some children love to write poetry because many of the "rules" don't apply! Not all children like writing poetry, however. Don't expect **all** your second graders to enjoy this lesson or assignment if you choose to do a focused writing lesson with it.

The teacher talks about what she will write, then writes two examples:

Leaves	Lake
Colorful, crisp	Large, lovely
Waving, floating, falling	Boating, fishing, swimming
Wonderful to watch any time	I love lake looking
Leaves	Water

The teacher reads the cinquains, then reads the directions and discusses what she has written and why.

She discusses the many topics the children could write about: books, storybook characters, friends, topics in school, etc.

The teacher points out that each line starts with a capital letter, but does not always end with punctuation. She stretches out **cr-is-p** and **won-der-ful** and gets them right. The teacher says, "I know how to spell words like: **float**, **fall**, **boat**, **fish**, and **swim** and then add the **ing**." She looks at the Editor's Checklist and tells how these items apply to writing poetry.

Other Ideas for Writing Poetry

Writing Acrostic Poetry with the Children's Names

One mini-lesson you can do is to model an acrostic poem using a child's name. This can follow a lesson on adjectives or can be done when talking about the children.

Marvelous
Imaginative
Charming
Happy
Energetic
Lively
Lovely
Eager

Writing Acrostic Poetry with Storybook Characters' Names

Model for the children how you write a character's name from a book you have read. Then, find examples from the book in each letter of the name. Example:

Never bored when he is around
A good detective
The boy who is always solving mysteries
Enemy of the bad guy

Writing Biography Poems

Biography poems can be written by children about themselves. Use your name, your child's name, or a child's name in the class as an example:

(Name/ Title)	Ashleigh
(Describe yourself)	Happy, daughter, pretty
(What do you like?)	Lover of dogs, books, and pizza
(How do you feel?)	Who feels lucky sometimes
(What do you fear?)	Who fears snakes, insects, and spiders
(What would you like to do?)	Who likes to visit her Grandma and Grandpa
(Where do you live?)	Resident of Michigan
(Name, and/or nickname)	Ashleigh

Mini-Lesson Focus: Modeling Revision Using Think-Alouds

Second grade teachers are usually comfortable editing with young children. They like to edit because they know what to do. Teachers find it easy to find the missing capital letters and fix the wrong punctuation marks at the end of sentences. Teachers can recognize misspelled words and can correct them. Most teachers are not as comfortable with revision. They often wonder how much you should ask young children to revise their writing and how much revision to teach to emergent writers. Second graders shouldn't be expected to do much revision, but most second graders can learn to reread what they have written and think about how to make it better. As with all writing skills, the best way to teach revision is by modeling, modeling, modeling! Here is a mini-lesson that focuses on revision:

The teacher reads a piece she has chosen to publish and asks children to help her make it clearer and more interesting:

Myrtle Beach

One of my favorite places to visit is Myrtle Beach. It is in South Carolina. I go there once every year—sometimes more! I like to sit in the sand and build sand castles. I like to ride the ocean waves into the shore. I like to go a restaurant to eat seafood. I like to shop at all the shops. Sometimes I get to go to a show or ride the rides. Going to the beach is fun!

The teacher asks children some questions:

"Does my piece have a good beginning?"

"Is there anything you think I need to add?"

"Is everything in the right order?"

"Does it have a good ending?"

"Can you think of anything that would make this piece better or more interesting?"

The teacher thinks aloud about the children's responses and revises her piece:

If the children think it needs a better beginning (and the teacher agrees), then the teacher helps the class write a better introductory sentence. If the children want to know something ("How do you get there?"), she may add another sentence or two (It is a long drive for my family from our home to the coast.). Thinking about each question helps her look at the writing and offers a chance to "make it better" by adding on (I like to shop at all the shops on the boardwalk), changing a word, changing the order of the sentences, or adding something to the end (Going to Myrtle Beach is always fun!).

Other Ideas for Modeling Revision Using Think-Alouds

Teaching Revision by Starting with a Good Sentence

Many children have little trouble writing good sentences at the beginnings of their writing. For other children, this can be a problem! Good writing "hooks" the reader or listener from the start. Starting a story or an informational piece with a strong introductory sentence is important. Look through your students' writing to find a good piece that does not start with a good sentence. Help the child change it in a class mini-lesson.

Birds

In spring we see birds.

This piece starts with a sentence about one thing we see in spring. Ask the writer why he chose to write about birds. Use his answer to help him come up with one or two new beginning sentence possibilities.

Spring is back, so are the birds.

Teaching Revision by Adding On ("Tell Me More!")

Remember the song from the musical and movie *Grease* —it went something like this "Tell me more, tell me more, ..." Some children start writing and stay on topic but do not tell us enough. They need to tell us more. We can encourage them to "tell us more" by singing this little song to them! Do a mini-lesson with the writing of several children who are getting ready to publish. This is also a good technique to use when conferencing with individual children.

Teaching Revision by Putting Things in the Right Order or Sequence

Often young children tell the whole story but don't tell it in the right order. They tell the events as they remember them. Helping children to put the events in the right sequence will make their writing easier to understand for those who will read it.

Teaching Revision by Combining Sentences

Often writers have too many sentences and need to combine some. One child wrote:

My mother likes picking berries. My father likes picking berries.
My sister likes picking berries. I like picking berries.

A partner reading the story suggested that she combine the sentences and write:

My mother, father, sister, and I like picking berries.

The child decided to write:

My family likes picking berries. So do I.

Mini-Lesson Focus: Writing Is Like Juggling

Writing, like reading, is a complex cognitive process. Children have many things to remember, or juggle, when writing. Children must think of topics that they want to tell about and what exactly they want to tell. They must think about capital letters, ending punctuation, good handwriting, how to spell many words, and how to stretch out other words. Teachers who are most successful at teaching writing look at what their children are doing and let the children's daily writing tell them what they need to teach. We can't cover everything a child needs to know about writing every day. Occasionally, however, we do a lesson in which we think aloud about all the "balls a writer must juggle."

The teacher thinks aloud and writes about:

Choosing a Topic

"I could write about my best friend. We all have good friend we like to write about. I could write about all the flowers I planted in my back yard yesterday after school. I thought since we were planting flowers at school, I should plant some at home. But, I think I will write about Encyclopedia Brown—the detective in the chapter book I am reading to you. You all like him so much I thought that would be a good topic."

Narrowing the Topic

"I could write a summary of the story with a beginning, middle, and end. I could tell you why I like this book. I really like mysteries, especially when the main character is a detective just your age! I think I will tell you why I like Encyclopedia Brown books."

Writing a Good Sentence Using Capital Letters, Spelling, and Punctuation Marks

"My first sentence is: 'Encyclopedia Brown is a detective.'. Both **Encyclopedia** and **Brown** need a capital letter. I know how to spell his name by looking at the cover of the book. **Detective** is not on the Word Wall or in the room so I will stretch that word out and write the sounds I hear: **de-tec-tive**. I remember to put a period at the end of the sentence because it is a telling sentence."

Staying on Topic, Stretching Out Words, and Using Beginning Capitals and Correct Ending Punctuation

"My next sentence tells why I like the book." The teacher writes:

> I like mysteries; especially mysteries with a detective who is the same age as the children in this class.

"I begin with a capital letter because sentences begin with capital letters. I know how to spell **like**, **with**, and **who** because they are on the Word Wall. **Name** is on the Word Wall so I change **n** to **s** and I write **same**. I know how to write **mystery** but to write **mysteries** I have to change the **y** to **i** and add **es**. **Children**, **this**, and **class** are on the Word Wall, too. (By the end of the year, many words the children need are there!) Continue writing and thinking aloud as you write.

Most days we focus our mini-lesson on one point. This mini-lesson reminds children of all the thinking a writer does. Writing really is like juggling!

Other Ideas for Writing Is Like Juggling

What to Do When You're "Stuck" . . . One More Time

All writers occasionally have trouble thinking of something to write about. (Even teachers have that problem!) The children need to know that all writers and authors get "writer's block" when they are not sure what to write about next. A writer or author might take a break when this happens but would never just stop writing. Look at your list of "Topics We Could Write About" on the wall or in your writing notebook or folder. Another idea is to look around the room to get ideas. Model this. For example, the teacher might look up at a stuffed rabbit and be reminded of a "story" about a stuffed rabbit that comes to life. The teacher might look at some crayons and be reminded of the time she used her crayons to draw a picture on her bedroom wall and got into trouble! Look at the flag and remember a time the United States won a gold medal at the Olympics and the flag was raised during the award ceremony at the end. Then, write and model everything writers have to remember (and juggle!).

Getting Your Thoughts on Paper . . . Students Can Help

Sometimes you know what to write about but have trouble getting your thoughts on paper. Model this for your students and ask them to help you. "I went to watch Ashleigh and Andrew play Little League last night. I want to write about it but I don't know much about playing baseball. Will those of you who know all about Little League help me?" This is the perfect time for the children to do a shared or interactive writing mini-lesson. Remind the students of all the things they need to know, besides knowing about Little League, to help you write this story.

Juggling Spelling

By the fourth quarter of the year, most second-grade classrooms have about 120 words on the Word Wall. Our daily Word Wall practice and review helps everyone know which words are on the wall and where the words are. Children do need to be reminded, however, to refer to the Word Wall, theme boards, and charts in the room and use them! They also need to hear us model other ways to spell words that we practice during Working with Words—adding **s** to nouns for plurals and to make verbs sound right, adding **er** and **est** to words, and changing beginning letters to spell new words that rhyme with Word Wall words and many times changing a beginning sound and adding an ending. Mini-lessons on the different ways we spell words as we write need to be continued throughout the second grade year.

Juggling Grammar

We introduce writing to children by telling them that writing is telling. As the year goes on, however, we want children to learn that sometimes we don't write things exactly the way we say them. Many children say, "My friend and me went to the movie." Asking children, "Does that sound right?" doesn't help. One little second grader responded, "Sounds right to me!" and he was right, it did sound right to him. That was just the way he and his friends said it. If writing is like telling, we need to let them write as they talk—except when we are "making it public." If the student is not publishing, we do not correct grammar. When a piece of writing is being published, however, we correct grammar by simply saying, "That is a way to say it. But when we write it, we write is this way. Late in second grade, many teachers do mini-lessons in which they correct the grammar in a piece that is about to be published by making the "way we say it—way we write it" distinction.

Mini-Lesson Focus: Writing Stories (Making a Class Book)

Most second graders write about things they know in their "all-about" stories. Second grade children write all about their friends, all about their dog, all about a favorite game they watched, etc. They tell "real" stories instead of making up stories and writing "fiction." Second graders usually write stories with a beginning, a middle, and an end when we teach that in reading and model it during writing. Later in the year when most of the students are writing well (for second graders!), teachers often do a focused-writing lesson on stories. They model writing a story for the mini-lesson and then the children all write stories. Here is an example focused on a special day in second grade.

The teacher tells what she will write about and then writes her story:

" We have had many good days in second grade. I remember the first day when we were all new to each other and the days when new students came to our class. I remember a lot of birthdays—even the day I told you it was my birthday! I remember the fall festival, our Thanksgiving feast, our Valentine's Day party, and all the days we had visitors. I remember the assemblies we have watched and the books we have read. Today I am going to tell you a story about one special day in second grade. This is a true story; it really happened. My story about a special day in second grade will have a beginning, a middle, and an end. Watch and see what I have chosen to write about." (It could take multiple days to write, revise, and edit as she leads the class through a focused-writing assignment.)

The teacher writes the beginning:

The First Day of Second Grade

I remember the first day of second grade. I didn't know you and you didn't know me. We learned each other names quickly. We started the day with a class meeting. I read a favorite book to you. I showed you some different books I . . .

She has the children read the beginning with her, discusses it, and then writes the middle.

Next, we talked about the different books we would read in Guided Reading and we previewed my book collections together. Then, I wrote about myself and when it was your time to write many of you wrote about yourself. At math time . . .

The teacher has the children read the middle with her, discuss it, and write the end.

After lunch, we talked about the themes we would study in second grade. We talked about places we would go on field trips. It was hot when we played outside. The last thing I did was review our day and write about it.

"We have had many good days together since then. That is what I want you to write about today—a special day you remember in second grade. When you finish these stories, we will edit and publish them, and put them in a class book. I will make copies of the book for everyone to take home so you can remember your friends and second grade and your parents can see the personal narratives you have written in second grade!"

The teacher discusses which day each child might like to write about as she dismisses them to go back to their seats and write one by one.

The teacher starts with children who already know what they will write about and have their hands raised and a happy, confident look on their faces. "What day are you going to write about, Suzanne?" ("The day we decorated gingerbread houses.") "Ryan?" ("The day the man from the Nature Science Center brought snakes to school!") "DaSawndra?" ("The day I made my first book.") Continue like this so that you know every child has something to write about and they are not all the same. If a child does not have an idea, help him come up with one.

Working on this focused lesson will take some time.

Most children need several days to write the stories while the teacher circulates, encourages, and helps. Next, the stories need to be self-edited and peer edited, and then edited by the "chief editor"— the teacher! Then, the stories need to be typed on the computer (perhaps by a parent volunteer). Finally the stories need to be published by duplicating them for the whole class and binding them together in a class book.

What do the children do if they finish their story before other children? Return to self-selected topics!

Other Ideas for Writing Stories (Making a Class Book)

Writing Fiction

Young children like to tell true stories, but making up one is harder. Some children do make up stories. These children are usually familiar with how stories are written because someone has read to them since they were young. Second grade teachers need to model fiction by making up a story and writing this in a mini-lesson.

"I am thinking about how many of the stories we read are written. Sometimes they begin, 'Once upon a time,' or 'In a far away place,' or they tell where the story takes place and what it is like. I will begin that way."

In a little village on the coast lived a boy named Daniel. The boy was no ordinary boy. In his back yard was a magic treehouse . . . .

Writing Team Stories

Second graders love to work on teams. Divide the class into teams or groups. Give each team or group time to write the beginning of a story together. Have them edit it because another team will read it tomorrow. Make sure the stories are readable before the next day. The next day, each team reads the beginning of another team's story and adds a middle. On the third day, each group gets a story they haven't seen before and adds an ending. You may need to assign the writer who will do the actual writing for each group. This should be someone who can write quickly and legibly so everyone can read it.

Mini-Lesson Focus: Writing a "How to" Class Book

Young children like to tell how to make things. (Sometimes their writing makes the local newspaper because their directions are very entertaining!) Teaching mini-lessons on writing directions helps children focus on sequencing. In this lesson, children make peanut butter-oatmeal no-bake cookies. After making and enjoying their snack, the teacher and class compose directions for making these cookies. The following day, children write favorite recipes for a Mother's Day cookbook.

Teacher thinks aloud about what to write:

"We have just finished making and eating peanut butter-oatmeal cookies. Now let's write about it. What did we do first? Yes, we mixed together a stick of margarine, $1/2$ cup of cocoa, a cup of sugar, and $1/2$ cup of milk. Then, we cooked that on our hot plate until we saw bubbles around the sides."

Peanut Butter-Oatmeal No-Bake Cookies

First, we gather the ingredience: (Be sure to stretch this out)

(1 stick of margarine, $1/2$ cup cocoa, 1 cup sugar, $1/2$ cup milk, $1/2$ cup peanut butter, 3 cups quick oats.)

Next, we mix together the margarine, cocoa, sugar and milk.

Then, we cook the mix until it bubbles.

Finally, we add the peanut butter and oatmeal and mix.

We drop the cookies onto wax paper and let them cool.

Then the best part comes. We get to eat them!

The teacher talks about other sandwiches, casseroles, cookies, and snacks the children make or someone makes for them: "I know you eat a lot of sandwiches. I could write about making a grilled cheese sandwich. Have you ever made brownies? They are fun and easy to make. My children like me to make nachos and cheese. I have a special recipe for that. Do you have a favorite dish you help your mother with?"

The teacher lets the children tell about their favorite recipes and whether or not they know how they make them, then records their list:

grilled cheese	BLTs	s'mores
blueberry muffins	tacos	salad
macaroni and cheese	potato soup	chocolate chip cookies
zucchini bread	brownies	corn bread
peanut butter and jelly sandwiches		

On the following day, the teacher has children write down the directions for making their favorite recipe. She lets children who brought in the same recipe write together.

The teacher edits, illustrates, and compiles these recipes. She duplicates a **Favorite Recipes** cookbook for everyone in the class to take home.

Other Ideas for Writing a "How to" Class Book

Doing a Science Experiment, then Having Students Write about What They Did

In Four-Blocks classrooms we try to integrate as much as possible. We like to tie our writing to the things we are learning in Social Studies and Science. "Yesterday we planted seeds that will grow into plants. (They may be our Mother's Day presents!)"

Planting Marigolds

Yesterday we planted marigold seeds. First, we put dirt in a paper cup. Next, we poked three holes in the dirt. Then, we put the marigold seeds into those holes. Finally we watered the seeds and put our cups in the sunshine in the windows. We will watch the seeds grow into marigolds!

Writing about Learning How to Do Something

Write about learning to ice skate or roller skate, ride a bike, water ski or snow ski, or learning to swim. Tell the class how you learned to do it and let them tell you how they learned. Emphasize that order is important and transition words help tell what you did when.

Skating

Our school has skate night once a month. Everyone likes to go skating. I learned to skate when I was young. We skated outside on the sidewalk. Back then skates were metal and fastened to your shoes. First, you . . . .

Have the children tell how they learned to roller skate, ice skate, ride a bike, swim, etc.

Writing about How to Play a Sport or Game

Talk about your favorite outside (soccer) or inside (Monopoly) game. Write about it.

Monopoly

It seems like everyone has played Monopoly at one time or another. It is a popular board game. The board has streets, railroads, and public companies around the edge. Each player picks a . . . .

Writing about How to Draw a Person (Face, House, Animal, etc.)

Combine art and writing. Draw a picture of a person's face. Write about how you do this. Have the children draw pictures and write about how they drew these objects. Let the children read their directions to a partner. See if the partner can follow the directions.

Mini-Lesson Focus: Young Authors' Celebration

The focus of a good writing program in second grade is on children as authors. Setting aside time for children to share their writing is an important part of the writing process. It also gives students the opportunity to develop listening and speaking skills. After writing each day, the children get to share their writing with the other students in an Author's Chair format. This is a time when some children get ideas for stories they too can write. ("I have a bike in my garage. I can write about riding **my** bike." "I went to the lake to fish with my friend Jimmy. I could write about that." "I got a neat game for **my** birthday. I could tell about that.")

Publishing is an important part of children's daily writing even in second grade. When publishing, children find a real reason to look at their writing and revise ("make it better"), edit ("make it right") and publish ("make it public"). When you do not try to take every piece the children write to final copy, publishing is a more reasonable process.

We can let children have an even wider audience at a "Young Authors' Celebration". The last month of school is a good time for students to do this. If your students have been making books throughout the year, they can simply choose one of their books, read it, and see if they can make it better (Draw the pictures better, find a "typo" or a place where they did not recopy the editing correctly, or make a newer, nicer cover.)

If you have not been publishing but your students have been writing in notebooks, folders, or you have been saving some writing on computer disks, then you already have the pieces that will become your books. Tell the class about the upcoming Young Authors' Celebration and about the books they will share with family and friends.

The teacher thinks aloud about her writing:

"These are some books (pieces) I have written. Let me read them and see which one I like the best; or which one I think other people might like." Then, read two or three of your books. Since you have not been publishing all year like the students have, you may not have as many books as the children in your class (most teachers do not!). Instead, read two or three pieces of writing. Talk about what you like about each piece and what you think other people would like about it. "I think people might like my piece about picking berries. I wrote that after reading Gail Gibbons's *The Berry Book.* Lots of people like berries and some people pick berries just like me. I like my Martin Luther King, Jr. piece. I did a good job telling about his life. Another favorite is "**Camping Out**." But I do not think that would be everyone's favorite. I think I would like to make my piece about picking berries into a book for our Young Authors' Celebration."

Next the teacher goes through the publishing steps on pages 44 and 45.

Choose a book to put the writing in—many teachers have parents help bind enough books for all the children in the class to use for Young Authors' Celebration and then put the children's writing into these blank books. Other teachers have parents "bind" the books after the children finish with them. In each book you need: the back and front cover, a title page, dedication page, 5 to 10 pages for the student's writing, and an author page.

If you have computers, decide how you can get these stories typed and printed. If they are written in the children's best handwriting that is fine, too!

Getting ready for a "Young Authors' Celebration" will take time, so plan ahead.

Other Ideas for Young Authors' Celebrations

Writing Invitations to the Young Authors' Celebration or Tea

Tell the students about invitations and have them help you write a class invitation to the Young Authors' Celebration. Let the students copy this for their handwriting lesson and take the invitations home to their family members.

You are invited to our Young Authors' Celebration

Who: Family and Friends

When: May 12, 2003 at 2:00 P.M.

Where: Room 22, South Haven Elementary

We hope you can come!

Writing about What Will Happen at the Young Authors' Celebration

Talk about that day and what will happen. Children need to know what will happen at their "Young Authors' Celebration" and what they are expected to do. By doing this mini-lesson you will prepare your children for the events.

The Young Authors' Celebration

First we will divide into four groups. Each group will have a leader and a special place in the room. Then, we will read our books to our parents, family, and friends. Finally we will have a tea. The children will serve the adults. We will have punch, cookies, and nuts. It will be fun!

Writing about How Your Class Will Read Their Books

Think aloud, tell, and write about how your class will read their books.

During our Young Authors' Celebration we will divide into four groups to read our books. That way everyone can read their books and everyone can hear others read. Remember to practice reading so you will do a good job. You can clap after each book (or at the end—you decide!).

Having Your Students Share with Other Second-Grade Classes

Some teachers feel that a big celebration is not what they want but they want to share their student's writing beyond the classroom. Sharing with the other second-grade classes is one way to do this. How many second grades? Each teacher divides the students in their class by that number. Three classes means divide the classes in thirds and each teacher has a "sharing" time with 1/3 of each class.

Having Your Students Share with Older (or Younger) Children

Send your students to another, older grade level to read their writing. Example: Pair with the fourth-grade teachers and send 1/3 (if there are three classes) of your students, with their books, to each of the classrooms.

References

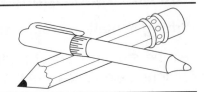

Professional References

Calkins, L. M. (1994) *The Art of Teaching Writing.* Portsmouth, NH: Heinemann Publishing.

Cunningham, P. M.; Hall, D. P.; and Cunningham, J. W. (2000) *Guided Reading the Four-Blocks® Way.* Greensboro, NC: Carson-Dellosa Publishing, Co.

Cunningham, P. M.; Hall, D. P.; and Gambrell, L. B. (2002) *Self-Selected Reading the Four-Blocks® Way.* Greensboro, NC: Carson-Dellosa Publishing, Co.

Cunningham, P. M.; Hall, D. P.; and Sigmon, C. M. (1998) *The Teacher's Guide to the Four-Blocks®.* Greensboro, NC: Carson-Dellosa Publishing, Co.

Hall, D. P. and Cunningham, P. M. (1997) *Month-by-Month Phonics for Second Grade.* Greensboro, NC: Carson-Dellosa Publishing, Co.

Children's Books Cited

Alexander, Who Used to be Rich Last Sunday by Judith Viorst (Atheneum, 1978).

Arthur Makes the Team by Marc Brown (Little, Brown and Co., 1998).

Arthur's Pet Business by Marc Brown (Little, Brown and Co., 1993).

The Berry Book by Gail Gibbons (Holiday House, 2002).

Curious George Series by H. A. Rey (Houghton Mifflin, Co.).

Encyclopedia Brown Series by Donald J. Sobol (Bantam Skylark).

How I Spent My Summer Vacation by Mark Teague (Dragonfly, 1997).

Ira Sleeps Over by Bernard Waber (Houghton Mifflin, Co., 1973).

The Jolly Postman or Other People's Mail by Janet and Allan Ahlberg (Little, Brown and Co., 2001).

Junie B. Jones Series by Barbara Parke (Random House).

Magic Tree House Series by Mary Pope Osborne (Random House).

Missing: One Stuffed Rabbit by Maryann Cocca-Leffler (Albert Whitman and Co., 1998).

Miss Nelson Is Missing by Harry Allard (Houghton Mifflin, Co., 1977).

My Great-Aunt Arizona by Gloria Houston (HarperCollins, 1992).

The Relatives Came by Cynthia Rylant (Atheneum, 2001).

Stellaluna by Janelle Cannon (Scholastic, 1993).

The True Story of the Three Little Pigs by Jon Scieszka (Scholastic, 1989).